— Burghley House —

BURGHLEY HOUSE

John Martin Robinson · Photographs by Ashley Hicks

Foreword by Miranda Rock

RIZZOLI
NEW YORK
New York · Paris · London · Milan

— Contents —

— Foreword —

WITH THE RECENT CELEBRATIONS for the 500th anniversary of the birth of William Cecil, there has never been a more poignant time to reflect on the remarkable survival of this great house. Cecil's ambitions were visionary: Burghley represented a dynastic seat of permanence that he hoped would endure for future generations. I have no doubt that he and his descendants would be both delighted and amazed that his house continues to thrive. This is thanks not only to the prudence and farsightedness of generations of custodians—but also to the legions of men and women who have lived and laboured amongst them.

Burghley may be described as a house, but it is actually more like a village—and this is as true today as it was in the sixteenth century. It is an incredible privilege to grow up and then work in a community where you feel both a profound connection to its past and a shared belief in its future. The extraordinary team of more than 150 dedicated and skilled staff working here today quite rightly share a passion for Burghley and a pride in what it stands for.

With amazing prescience, my grandfather David, 6th Marquess of Exeter, created a charity to preserve in perpetuity the house, collections and surrounding estate that will ensure that Burghley remains secure and can continue to be enjoyed by hundreds of thousands of visitors every year. With an emphasis on education, environmental sustainability, and in support of local community, his ambitions have never felt more relevant.

This book is a celebration of each and every generation who has lived at Burghley. Some have left their extravagant mark, others have necessarily lived a more prudent tenure which was equally important. But all have been instrumental in preserving and embellishing the magical place we see today.

Creating this beautiful book has been a fascinating journey and it has been a privilege to work with John Martin Robinson, Ashley Hicks and Robert Dalrymple in bringing it to fruition. Special thanks are due to Orlando, for his expertise and eye for detail; to Jon Culverhouse, Curator at Burghley, for his patient research; and most importantly to the Governors of the Burghley House Preservation Trust, for their dedication and ongoing support now and for the next 500 years.

This book is a celebration of all the family, staff, trustees, volunteers, visitors, experts, friends and enthusiasts who enable Burghley to continue to flourish... and it is dedicated to them with love and pride.

MIRANDA ROCK · 2025

[1] *opposite* Orlando and Miranda Rock with (left to right) Jemima, Lila, Matilda and Cosmo Rock.

Giulio Romano
2

CHAPTER I

— Lord Burghley's Prodigy House —

EXTERNALLY BURGHLEY HOUSE REMAINS largely as it was conceived in the sixteenth century by the 1st Lord Burghley (1520–1598), William Cecil, Principal Secretary (from 1558) and Lord Treasurer to Queen Elizabeth I (from 1572)—the man who guided the destinies of England for forty years up to his death in 1598. He was the Queen's 'Principal Servant' and trusted partner in power for all that time and helped to create modern England with its compromise national church and strong mercantile economy. He was also the greatest builder of the age. The Queen herself built little, as she had inherited too many palaces from her father, Henry VIII; she liked to spend the summers on Progresses to different parts of the country staying with her chief nobles who were expected to make their houses worthy of the honour and to entertain her royally. As a result, her courtiers were the leading architectural patrons of her reign, and William Cecil was the head of the pack.

He built two enormous principal houses, Theobalds in Hertfordshire close to London and Burghley House at Stamford in the Midlands, as well as other works. Theobalds was a new estate acquired by him, intended primarily as a place to entertain the Queen. In Lord Burghley's own words, it 'was begun by me with a mean measure but encreast by occasion of her majesty's often coming'. She visited Theobalds no fewer than thirteen times and treated it as if it was one of her own palaces. With the Queen in mind, Lord Burghley created a vast residence there, planned around three courtyards, with state rooms for the Sovereign, and accommodation for Royal Household officials like the Lord Chamberlain. Theobalds descended to Robert Cecil, the Lord Treasurer's son by his second marriage, who swapped it for Hatfield with James I, and it was destroyed in the Civil War.

Burghley House was also the residence of a 'chief minister thinking royally', though not quite on the same scale as Theobalds. Queen Elizabeth only visited once when the place was in its early stages and she and the court stayed in Stamford because of a suspected smallpox outbreak in the Cecil household. Burghley House, like Theobalds, was built with state rooms for the reception of the monarch as well as separate accommodation for the family, and this has determined its character down to the present day. State rooms were occasionally occupied by royalty and have always been largely public showplaces, while the ground floor family rooms have been continuously occupied over the centuries by Lord Burghley's descendants. The emphasis at Burghley was, however, different from William Cecil's at Theobalds; the Lord Treasurer saw Burghley primarily as the seat of his title and dynasty on the site where his family had their roots. In his own phrase, it was to make the point that he was not a 'new-feathered lord'. One of the striking aspects of Burghley House is that Lord Burghley in his prime hardly lived there and rarely visited it, as he was mainly occupied with affairs of state in London or building—and then entertaining the Queen at Theobalds. His mother lived at Burghley during her lifetime, and then his eldest son, Thomas Cecil, used it as his own house and ran the estate on the spot from the 1560s onwards.

Nevertheless, Lord Burghley was involved in every detail of the design, discussing features, making drawings himself, directing the works and generally acting as his own architect. At Burghley he was looking back, stressing his family connection in the area, enhancing that historic connection with newly minted heraldry from the College of Arms, and looking forward by creating a suitable seat for the noble dynasty he himself had founded and of which the new house he erected was to be the architectural embodiment. His coronet and Garter were prominent in the decoration of its later stages. In this, William Cecil was characteristic of the 'new men' and women of Tudor England like Sir John Thynne, his old ally in the circle of the Protector Somerset, at Longleat, or Bess of Hardwick in Derbyshire, who both

COR VNVM VIA VNA

[2] *previous pages* The skyline of Lord Burghley's house; an array of turrets, chimneys, obelisks, and heraldry.

[3] *opposite* Attributed to Marcus Gheeraerts, William Cecil, 1st Lord Burghley KG, wearing Garter Robes and holding his white wand of office as Lord Treasurer, the principal office in the government of Queen Elizabeth.

[4] *right* Marcus Gheeraerts, Queen Elizabeth I in older age, richly dressed and bejewelled as 'Gloriana'.

erected spectacular dynastic houses which with Burghley form the supreme trinity of surviving English sixteenth-century domestic architecture.

William Cecil's background was typical of the emergent Tudor court–administrative nobility. Originally called Sitsilt and originating in the Welsh Marches, like other Welshmen—the Herberts, for instance—the Cecils had followed the Tudors to London and sought their fortune in the Royal Household. William's father and grandfather had both served Henry VII and Henry VIII in the lower echelons of the court. They prospered and bought lands in the Midlands including Burghley and property in Stamford, taking advantage of the fluid land market following sales of church estates. Lord Burghley's grandfather David was mayor of Stamford and established local prominence for the family there. Their rise in the world reached a spectacular culmination in William Cecil's own career as the principal royal official and holder of the two most lucrative court offices with enormous perquisites and emoluments. As Lord Treasurer from 1572 to 1598, he received a salary of £366 a year plus additional payments amounting to around £4,000 a year, derived from 'presents' from supplicants and interest on moneylending. He was also Master of the Court of Wards from 1561 onwards with responsibility for heirs whose fathers had died before their children had come of age. This post came with a salary of £133, but also the use of two thirds of the Wards' income during minorities which amounted generally to £3,000 per annum. This form of hybrid payment for great officials had been standard throughout Europe since the Middle Ages, and was economical for the state. It remained the norm in English government down to the Shelburne reforms of the late eighteenth century. Cecil's income was increased by many other official posts such as rangerships and wardenships of royal parks and castles, as well as leases and land deals. So from the 1560s up to his death, William Cecil had the income to build on a semi-royal scale.

He was sensitive to the criticism that his extravagant building and new wealth might attract and played it down, suggesting that Theobalds was a small house but had been expanded only for the Queen's benefit and accommodation, or that Burghley was really his mother's house and he was merely the tenant: 'My house of Burghley is of my mother's inheritance, who liveth, and is the owner thereof, and I but a farmer [tenant]; and for the building thereat I have set my walls on the old foundation. Indeed, I have made the rough stone walls to be squared and yet one side remaineth as my father left it to me.' This was written in 1585, before he embarked on rebuilding the north range, too, completing the majestic quadrangle that exists today. Nevertheless, some saw through the smokescreen. The poet Edmund Spenser wrote a satirical verse which without naming him was obviously aimed at the Lord Treasurer:

The cloak was care of thrift and husbandry,
For to increase the common treasure store;
But his own treasure he increased more,
And lifted up his lofty towers thereby
That begin to threat the neighbour sky . . .

[5] *left* Detail of a grisaille sixteenth-century wall painting of an architectural escutcheon, which gives an impression of the lost Elizabethan interior decoration.

[6] *right* Illuminated letters patent on vellum, dated 1571, of Queen Elizabeth I creating William Cecil the 1st Baron Burghley.

It was difficult for a house on the scale of Burghley with its skyline of turrets, ogee pepper pots, Doric column chimneystacks, obelisks and crestwork not to be noticed, for its architecture and design were meant to be extremely eye-catching! That was the point of Elizabethan house building on the large scale. It was intended to be prodigious. Burghley was a dynastic trumpet-blast on the grandest note possible, and it survives as the 'foremost expression of the sixteenth-century great house as the centre of political and dynastic power'.

In keeping with his architecture, William Cecil also ornamented his genealogy with classical detail. Thus, the change of name from Sitsilt to Cecil was partly a claim to Latin descent from the Ceciliae, a 'Roman tribe'. The general Renaissance-Italianisation of sixteenth-century Tudor culture saw the polishing of the English language from a guttural northern tongue like Dutch to one with a large Italian and Latin vocabulary and more elegant pronunciation with long Latinate vowels and softer consonants, more suited to sonnets, verse and a sonorous literature, immortalised by Shakespeare and the Authorised Version of the Bible, and which still determines educated English pronunciation today.

William Cecil's upbringing was that of a scholar, and he prepared for a career in public administration by a serious Renaissance education including Greek, Latin, philosophy and mathematics; studying at St. John's College, Cambridge, founded in 1511 by Lady Margaret Beaufort, mother of Henry VII and conduit of the royal claims of the Tudor dynasty, where he matriculated in 1535, and at Grays Inn, London, one of the Inns of Court, where he added Law to his intellectual armoury. He married as his first wife, Mary, the sister of John Cheke of St. John's College, a distinguished Greek scholar and his Cambridge tutor. His second wife, Mildred Cooke, was the sister of Edward VI's governor; her other sister was the mother of Francis Bacon, polymath-scholar and future Lord Chancellor of England.

When the child-king Edward VI succeeded his father Henry VIII, and his uncle the Duke of Somerset became King's Protector, the de facto ruler of England, William Cecil with his Cambridge credentials and Protestant sympathies became part of Somerset's governing group, acting briefly as his secretary and absorbing the architectural tastes of the Somerset circle. Cecil also became Chancellor of the Order of the Garter and was knighted in 1551 at the age of thirty-one. This rapid rise was halted by the execution of Somerset during the reign of Queen Mary and the seemingly successful English Counter-Reformation of Cardinal Pole, but with the accession of Queen Elizabeth I in 1558, Cecil became chief Secretary of State and helped establish the Elizabethan settlement in religion as a *via media* between Catholics and Protestants. He became the Queen's 'greatest, gravest, most esteemed Councillor' and remained so until death.

His father had bought the Burghley estate around the time William was born, and he built a house there of local stone which underlies the present structure. Whether

there had been an existing grange or farm on the site is not known, but Lord Burghley later referred to his father's house whose foundations he had used for his own work, proving that there was a place there from after 1520. William inherited this, with a life interest to his mother, in 1552, which gives a date for the commencement of the present Renaissance palace.

He started enlarging and remodelling at that time, and spent Queen Mary's reign quietly in the country engaged in building, a standard outlet for ambition in moments when the political tide in London was not flowing in the right direction, as with the 3rd Earl of Devonshire at Chatsworth after he fell out with James II, or William Aislabie, the Chancellor of the Exchequer at Studley Royal, after the South Sea Bubble burst. The house in the 1550s was already quadrangular with the Hall on the east side, but it was smaller, shaggier, and none of it is visible in the present sophisticated structure with its lofty elevations of smooth King's Cliffe ashlar stone. As with the later stages, there is no doubt even at the beginning that William Cecil was largely his own architect, a precursor of Lord Burlington's direct involvement with architecture in the eighteenth century, obtaining ideas and designs and presumably directing his masons. A letter in 1555 from his clerk of works describes French 'dormer' windows (a foreign fashion), the inner court, bay windows, the hall, its screen, and a gallery as being under construction. The kitchen roof is referred to as a major work still to be done. This was the inner range of the present east wing.

The adjoining Roman Stair is also thought to be of this date. The work in the house and gardens went on until 1564 when the mason Edmund Hall promised that the south range would be finished that winter in preparation for an expected visit from Queen Elizabeth who in the event did not stay. By then Cecil had bought Theobalds in Hertfordshire and transferred his architectural energies temporarily to the construction of that house from 1563 onwards. Burghley was occupied by William Cecil's mother, and then by his eldest son, Thomas Cecil (1542–1622), after the latter's marriage to Dorothy Neville, the daughter of Lord Latimer, and the birth of their eldest son, another William, in 1566.

[7] *below* Stone vaulting in the West Gatehouse, dated 1577, embellished with the Cecil family arms. The heraldry and the conscious reference to medieval gothic was a demonstration of Lord Burghley's noble status and genealogy. The architecture of Burghley House was that of a dynastic ancestral seat and was intended to show that William Cecil was not a 'new feathered lord'.

[8] *opposite* Drawing by John Haynes, 1755, of the inner courtyard before the addition of the early-nineteenth-century enclosed passages. The 1560s design is a masterpiece of English Renaissance architecture, with colonnades influenced by the Bourse in Amsterdam and a 'tower of the Orders', like Philibert de l'Orme's Château d'Anet in France, with correctly marshalled Doric, Ionic and Corinthian columns. The dramatic obelisk spire was an addition of 1585, and was later the inspiration for Hawksmoor's Christchurch, Spitalfields.

The Secretary of State was ennobled by the Queen in 1571, being raised to the peerage as 1st Lord Burghley and created a Knight of the Garter. This promotion rekindled William's interest in his ancestral base at Stamford as the seat of his new barony; construction began again on a much more ambitious scale than hitherto. In the meantime the creation of Theobalds on a palatial scale—influenced by Italian architects like Leon Battista Alberti and Sebastiano Serlio, or the Renaissance work of Francis I and Henry II at Fontainebleau, Chenonceau and Anet, and the engravings of the French architect and writer, Philibert de l'Orme (1514–1570)—had widened and informed Cecil's architectural ideas and ambitions. Theobalds provided a dry run for the more assured and sophisticated scheme that was now initiated at Burghley. The building team was reassembled, drawing on masons and craftsmen from the Royal Works in London, the doyens of their profession under the direction of Henry Hawthorne as clerk of works and then by John Symonds. Quarrying began at King's Cliffe to produce fine ashlar for the elevations. King's Cliffe was a royal park, and Lord Burghley enjoyed the role of Ranger there, one of his many positions that contributed towards his ambitious architectural project, in this case free building stone of the highest quality. With more ample resources, more experience of designing and building, and renewed vigour, Lord Burghley embarked on a new phase of complete reconstruction of his dynastic family seat.

Work continued throughout the 1570s and 1580s. The east wing was amplified into a double pile with the addition of a large new Great Hall, 68 feet long and 30 feet wide. This has a hammer-beam roof of oak and medieval three-tier form but with Renaissance decoration, and a striking Italianate stone chimneypiece dated 1573, derived from an engraving by Serlio. With the lofty stone-vaulted new kitchen and buttery built to the north-east of the screens end of the Hall, these additions were symbolic of a great nobleman's traditional duty of hospitality and therefore evoked Lord Burghley's new rank.

There followed the rebuilding of the west range further forward on a more regular alignment to which he was referring when he said he had made the 'rough stone walls to be square'. This enabled a large geometrical inner court and ceremonial axial approach to the 1560s east frontispiece. The house was transformed into a regular parallelogram of 240 feet by 125 feet, and three storeys high. The new symmetrical west front was the main entrance with flanking square bays like projecting towers and a tall turreted gatehouse in the centre alluding to the castle precedents of late medieval houses, and thus like the Great Hall redolent of lordly status. This ancestral aura was emphasised by a display of family heraldry to greet the visitor on the inner vault which is dated 1577 and gives the date of completion for the west

A Perspective View of the inner Court of Burghley House taken from the West End under the Arch near the Golden Gates, By I. Haynes A.D.MDCCLV.

side of the house. These three floors were intended for a long gallery and accommodation for guests.

There followed a reworking of the south range where there was an arcade on the ground floor opening to the gardens, with the intended royal apartments above—an arrangement similar to that at Theobalds. Finally, the north range was rebuilt with a dramatic bowed frontispiece like the prow of an Elizabethan galleon. It is dated 1587, a year before the defeat of the Spanish Armada which crowned the Queen's and Burghley's statesmanship with success and marked the high watermark of Elizabeth's reign. The north range was definitely designed by Lord Burghley himself, and sketch elevations for it in his own hand survive in the archives at Hatfield. It is clear from his correspondence that he often made 'trickes' and 'plattes' for his masons and surveyors to make up into proper drawings. This final part of the house contained separate apartments for Lord and Lady Burghley, an arrangement derived from royal palaces, and the central bow contained a summer banqueting room on the first floor overlooking the deer park with a private family entrance below.

The 1560s centrepiece of the east side of the courtyard, which gave entrance to the Great Hall, took the form of a 'tower of the Orders' with tiers of classical columns—Doric, Ionic and Corinthian like that designed by Philibert de l'Orme for the Château d'Écouen (and now at the École des Beaux Arts in Paris). This Roman triumphal arch was raised and made more prominent in the 1580s. The extra height added then was intended to make it echo the scale of the taller turreted west gatehouse of 1577. At this latter stage it was crowned by a clock tower supported by the Cecil heraldic beasts, small obelisks, and a central spire rising like a giant obelisk and dominating the whole composition close to and from afar. It is strangely akin to Hawksmoor's baroque treatment at Christ Church Spitalfields, just as Lord Burghley's heraldic animal supporters on either side seem to be precursors for Hawksmoor's lion and unicorn on the spire of St. George's Bloomsbury.[1] This showpiece is dated 1585.

[9] Charles Alfred Stothard (1786–1821), watercolour sketch of the west side of the courtyard in 1800, before the ground floor passages were added by the architect John Gandy Deering.

The crowning clock tower and obelisk spire contribute the most original and dramatic features of the Elizabethan architecture at Burghley. The Georgians saw this spire as the key focus of the whole spreading composition. William Gilpin, high priest of the Picturesque, wrote: 'at a distance . . . it contributes to give this immense pile the consequence of a town.'

The outer elevations of Burghley are relatively severe, symmetrical, and dominated by regular grids of large mullion and transom windows derived from English Perpendicular tradition, with fancy and embellishment largely being restricted to the turrets, chimneys and fretwork of the roof line. The interior courtyard by contrast was a complete set piece of joyous classical architecture with colonnades, applied Orders, Serliana, sculpture in roundels and arches. It is the greatest masterpiece of Franco-Flemish Elizabethan Renaissance architecture. Though part masked now by clever communication corridors added to the sides in the early nineteenth century, the original design can still be read clearly. It was a domestic parallel to Sir Thomas Gresham's Royal Exchange in the City of London. That is not a coincidence as Burghley and Gresham were friends, colleagues and connected by marriage, who shared tastes and interests in contemporary Continental architecture. Its bravura composition and informed use of the classical language makes it fully comparable with the sixteenth-century royal châteaux of the Loire in France. Horace Walpole in the eighteenth century called it 'beautiful scenery'. It is the finest surviving example of Elizabethan classical architecture.

William Cecil's architectural taste had been formed in the circle of the Protector when the latter was building Somerset House in London in 1547 up to the duke's execution in 1552. Many of the features that reappeared in John Thynne's Longleat and William Cecil's Burghley had first made their appearance at Somerset House, including fanciful skylines with columnar chimneys and entrance frontispiece with tiered Classical Orders derived from Serlio and large mullion and transom windows.

The most original and distinctive features of Lord Burghley's architecture are the Roman Stairs in the north-east corner of the house and the inner courtyard, both of which date from the 1560s, though the courtyard was only completed in the 1570s and 1580s. The Roman Stair was the first of its type in England with wide flights of stone steps rising between flanking walls under stone tunnel vaults. It derives from Italian practise as conveyed from France to Elizabethan England. Lord Burghley was much influenced by the publications and engravings of Philibert de l'Orme and Antonio Serlio who provided the sources for much of the classical detail. Despite its strong Franco-Italian character, the Roman Stair was entirely the work of English stone masons, as proved by a recent study by Jennifer Alexander.[2] The large number of masons' marks show that around fifty masons worked successively on the stone for the stair of which the core team comprised eleven men. The same masons' marks can be found on other local buildings including Fotheringhay, Kirby Hall, Rothwell Market House and Apethorpe, showing that the stone masons at Burghley were all skilled Northamptonshire craftsmen. The sophisticated Renaissance design was Burghley's own, showing his study of Continental architectural publications. A particularly interesting and distinctive design feature is the stone barrel vault which had continuous geometrical fretwork patterns of circles and squares throughout the surfaces. This pattern is a leitmotif of Lord Burghley's work and can also be seen, for instance, in the soffits of the arches of the west gatehouse, or the archways in the Great Hall. The circles and squares in the staircase vaults contain shallow carved decoration of flowers such as roses alternating with heraldic motifs of cinquefoils, étoiles, rooks, castles and crescents. The castles for instance derive from a Cecil

[10] Watercolour sketch by Charles Alfred Stothard, 1800, of the dramatic roofscape of Burghley from the north-east, showing the distinctive chimneys in the form of grouped Doric columns and the ogee turrets which are a strong feature of the design. Charles was the son of Thomas Stothard; he painted these watercolours while his father was working on the Hell Staircase.

[11] Watercolour sketch by Charles Alfred Stothard, 1800, of the Roman stairs, which captures the spatial character of the Italianate stone tunnel-vaulted flights, the earliest of their type in England.

heraldic badge, while the crescents come from the Cheke arms of Lord Burghley's first wife. This recherché abstract heraldic decoration is again indicative of Lord Burghley's own hand, as heraldry was the study of an Elizabethan gentleman (beyond the grasp of a mason) and heraldic details in sixteenth- and seventeenth-century architecture therefore usually display the educated input of an owner not an artificer. Cecil was known for his strong interest in genealogy and heraldry, and for commissioning research from the College of Arms.

While the Roman Stair is entirely the work of English masons working to Burghley's ideas, the other great Renaissance set piece of the house, the inner courtyard completed in around 1564, is documented as having a Flemish input via Lord Burghley's friend, fellow architectural enthusiast and colleague Sir Thomas Gresham who was the English resident in Antwerp in the 1560s. Financial agent to the English Crown and Minister Plenipotentiary to the Duke of Parma, Spanish Viceroy, Gresham was the key financier of the Elizabethan age and played a role in developing the Elizabethan economy parallel to Burghley's statesman role at Court. Gresham is best known for building the Royal Exchange in the City of London to provide a focal entrepôt for English trade in the City, on the Continental model. His ambitions were wider than that, however, and his main aim was to reinforce the wool trade with Flanders, then the industrial heartland of Europe and England's principal export market. Wool, the wool trade, and increasingly woollen manufactures, were the mainstay of the developing English export economy from the fourteenth to the seventeenth centuries. English wool was considered the best quality in Europe, and for nearly two hundred years was exported to Flanders through a monopoly market, the Staple in Calais. England's last remaining territory in mainland France and the foothold for its continental trade was lost in the reign of Queen Mary when Calais was conquered by the French in 1558, whereupon the Staple moved from France to the Spanish Netherlands. Gresham's role in Antwerp, then the financial and mercantile capital of northern Europe, was to maintain and promote English trade with the Low Countries after the fall of Calais, and to build strong trading links between Flanders and the City of London and his new Exchange there modelled on the Bourse in Antwerp. Like Burghley, he had a strong personal interest in architecture and the new Italianate buildings being erected in Antwerp.

As early as 1563 Gresham was procuring articles for the building of Burghley House, from the Flemish architect-mason Hendrik van Paesschen. This is thought to have been preparation for the intended central courtyard and included the Roman Doric columns for the flanking ground floor colonnades there similar to those at Gresham's Royal Exchange in the City. The courtyard at Burghley is a cross between Somerset House, with its balustrades and Serlian features, like the dramatic arched centrepieces of the north and south sides, and the more Flemish character of Gresham's Royal Exchange with colonnades at ground level. The Royal Exchange was burnt in the Great Fire of London leaving Burghley as the best surviving example of this phase of English Renaissance architecture. The court at Burghley measured 115 feet by 80 feet, with a dramatic focus at the east end in the frontispiece with its tiers of Orders and Roman archway. But the fundamental proportions of all the court's architecture derived from the Orders, with accurately managed details like the moulded string-courses between the storeys. It shows the influence of Écouen and the Petit Château at Chantilly being constructed simultaneously by the Constable of France, Anne de Montmorency, which were well-known to advanced architectural patrons in England like Sir Thomas Smith of Hill Hall in Essex, Sir Henry Norris and Lord Burghley who corresponded amongst each other about Vitruvius, Philibert de l'Orme and other classical architectural sources. (Sir Thomas Smith, for instance,

[12] Charles Alfred Stothard, watercolour of the mid-sixteenth-century kitchen in 1800. Stothard's sketches are an evocative record of the Elizabethan architecture.

owned four editions of Vitruvius, the Roman architectural theorist.)

Hans Hendrik van Paesschen (*c.* 1513–1582) was the Italian-trained Antwerp architect-mason introduced to Cecil by Sir Thomas Gresham. Paesschen had designed the fortifications and triumphal arches, the Raadhuis (Town Hall), Oosterhuis and Hanseatic House in Antwerp, and more to the point the roughly contemporary Royal Exchange in London from 1566 to 1568. His work at Burghley falls into this context. He may also have worked for Cecil at Theobalds. All the carved stonework at the Royal Exchange was imported from Antwerp, and van Paesschen was involved in providing the monolithic stone columns and sculpture for the arcades which were transported ready-made from Antwerp.[3] The correspondence amongst Cecil's papers at Hatfield includes a reference to 'Henryk's plan for my bay window' proving that he was employed by Cecil as an architect, producing drawings for the work. A distinctive feature of the colonnades were the circular medallions in the spandrels containing busts of modern heroes such as the Emperor Charles v and Suleiman the Magnificent, but also classical figures like Aeneas, Hector, Paris, Thersites, Medea, Jason and Andromache, stressing the legendary classical origins of the Tudors and Cecils. Lord Burghley and his contemporaries saw themselves as Romans, and the true successors of the Roman Empire, as the descendants of the Province of Britannia which had survived in the Welsh Marches. The carved portrait heads in the courtyard were copied from antique medals and coins. Some of these were reset in the early nineteenth century in the reproduction side colonnades as part of John Gandy Deering's remarkably tactful addition of internal corridors which will be discussed later.

The employment of Hendrik in the courtyard merely emphasises Cecil's own dominant role in the design of Burghley over nearly four decades. He was assisted by a series of clerks and artificers whose names are recorded, but they were executants rather than the directing designers. From 1560 until his death in 1578, Cecil's faithful steward and bailiff at Burghley was Peter Kemp who supervised and paid the workforce and directed the construction of the courtyard. Henry Hawthorne, a mason, was also involved until his death in 1577, and John Symonds was another artificer from the Royal Works. For the last phase, Cecil's faithful surveyor and clerk of works was Richard Shute whose correspondence recording the progress of work begins in July 1578, and who supervised the construction of the new west range. The names of individual craftsmen, many of them from the Royal Works, are also recorded. And it is suggested that the Southwark sculptor Cornelius Cure who was almost certainly responsible for Burghley's magnificent tomb in Stamford St. Martin, the family church, may also have been employed at Burghley.

A key figure for what might be called the 'dynastic phase' of reconstruction in the 1570s and 1580s was Lord Burghley's eldest son by his first marriage, Thomas Cecil. After his marriage to Dorothy Neville (the daughter and heiress of the 4th Lord Latimer of Snape Castle in Yorkshire) he lived at Burghley, making it his home and running the estate. In his father's long absences in London and at Theobalds, it was Thomas who was in charge on the spot. He too was interested in architecture. As a young man he had been on a Grand Tour to northern Europe including time at the French Court. Lord Burghley, while disapproving of visiting Rome and the decadent south, was a proponent of the educational value of travel in France and Flanders.

While being overshadowed by his father both in the latter's lifetime and posthumously, Thomas Cecil was a personage in his own right, intelligent, educated and cultivated, who had seen military service in the Low Countries and was a member of the Privy Council. Thomas Earl of Exeter was as passionate about architecture as was Lord Burghley. Apart from supervising the building and

[13] *right* Vellum plan of the layout of Exeter House, Strand, London. This was Lord Burghley's townhouse, redeveloped as streets in the late seventeenth and eighteenth centuries.

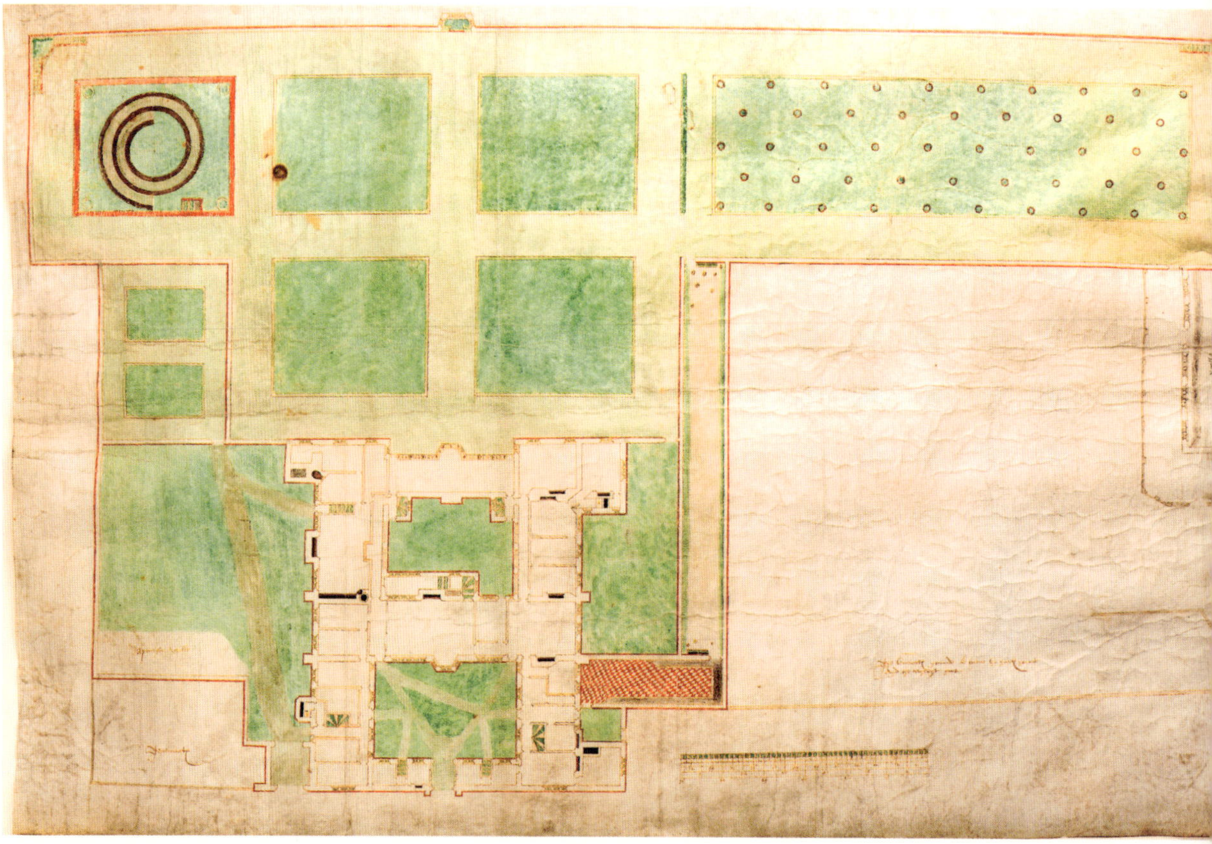

[14] *below* Wothorpe. A pavilion built on the Burghley estate by the 1st Earl of Exeter and a monument to his architectural enthusiasm. It has been a preserved ruin since the eighteenth century.

[15] *opposite* Circle of Marcus Gheeraerts the Younger (1561–1636), *Portrait of Thomas Cecil, 2nd Lord Burghley*, created 1st Earl of Exeter by James I in 1605. He shared his father's interest in architecture and had a strong influence on the development of Burghley House, where he lived in his father's lifetime.

completion of his father's work at Burghley House he also expressed his own architectural taste and knowledge in the fantastic Renaissance lodge he built at Wothorpe to the west of Burghley Park on the other side of the Great North Road, the shell of which with its geometrical plan, ogee turrets and Renaissance detailing still survives as an impressive feature in the local landscape.

Thomas was created Earl of Exeter in 1605, and a Knight of the Garter, by James I on the same day as his half-brother Robert was created Earl of Salisbury, establishing the two parallel Cecil dynasties: the Earls of Exeter, of Burghley, and the Earls of Salisbury, of Hatfield, both of whom were in due course to be raised to marquessates by George III, and both dynasties have lasted to the present day, together with their great houses. It is possible that Thomas, Earl of Exeter had a hand in the decoration of the Burghley state rooms in the 1580s which were remodelled by the 5th Earl at the end of the seventeenth century and are unrecorded but are known to have had decorative plaster ceilings, tapestry-hung walls and elaborate oak panelling, small sections of which survive in the little closets in the gatehouse turrets on the west front. The layout of the royal apartments on the south front, approached by a staircase at the east end, with a ceremonial progress through an enfilade of Presence Chamber, Privy Chamber, Bed Chamber, dressing room and closet underlies the current baroque enfilade of the George Rooms. The west

[16] John Thorpe, 1610, a record plan of the Ground Floor of Burghley House, commissioned by the 1st Earl of Exeter, showing the Great Hall with screens' passage, the kitchen at the top, and family apartments at the sides.

[17] John Thorpe, 1610, a record plan of the first floor of Burghley House with the original layout of Great Chamber on the right, and long gallery on the west before the 5th Earl's baroque remodelling between 1680 and 1700.

[18] *opposite* Views of the Elizabethan exterior: The east centrepiece of the courtyard and obelisk clock tower of Burghley House.

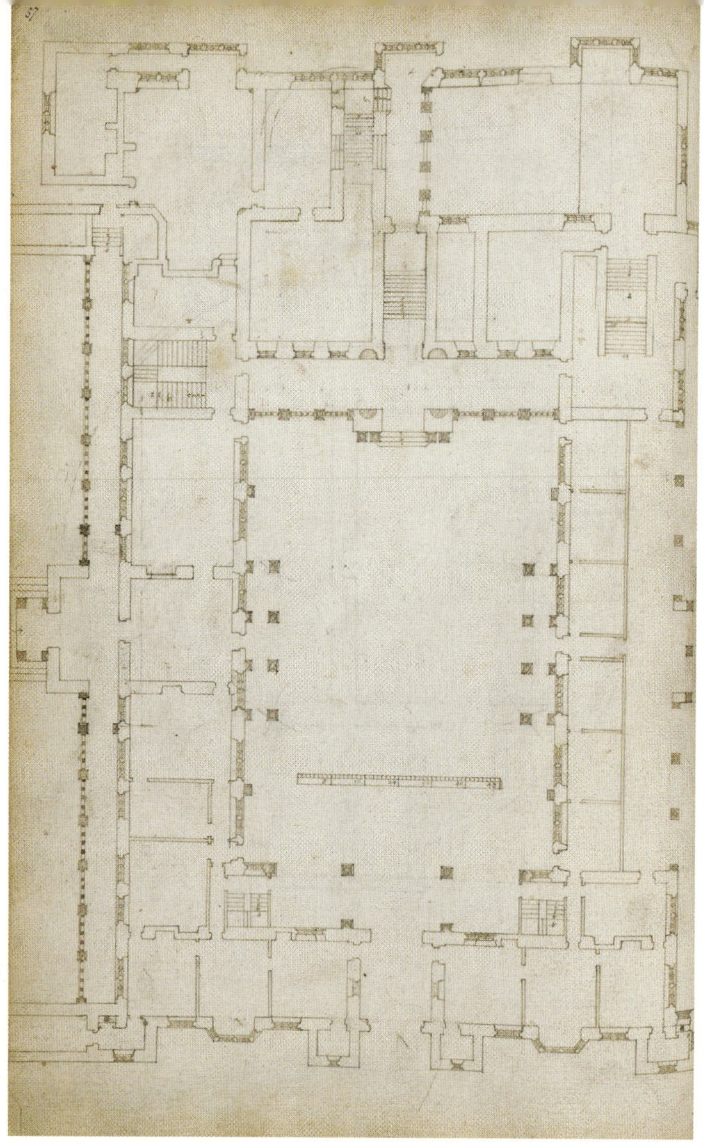

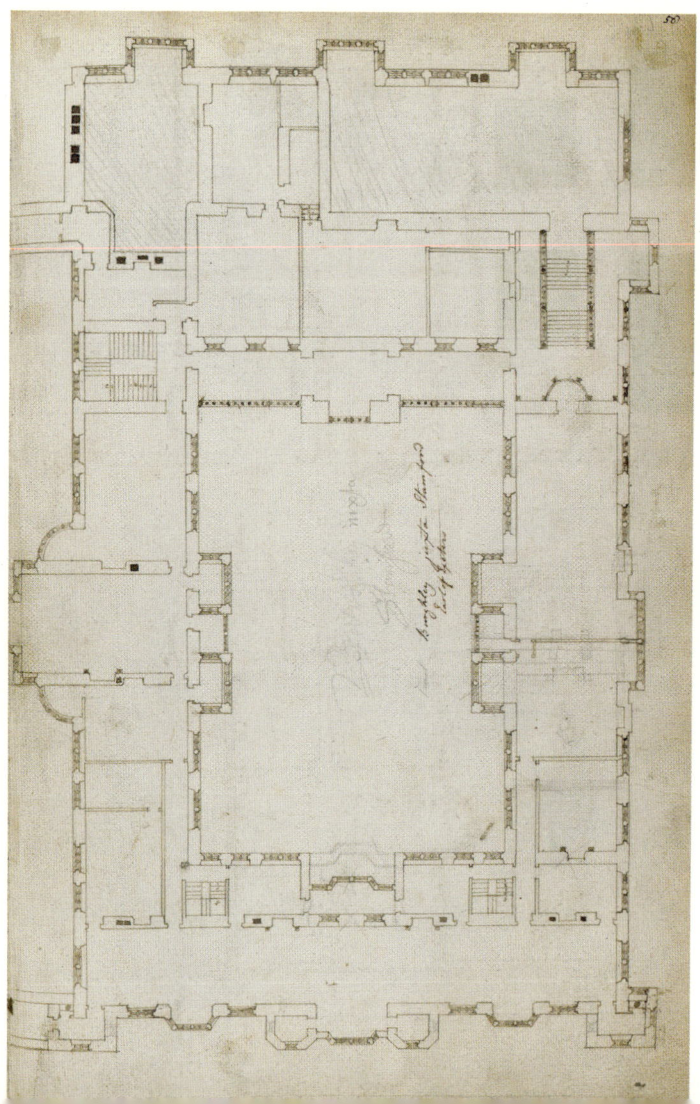

side comprised a long gallery on the first floor connecting to the family rooms in the north range. The name 'George Rooms' for the state apartments dates back to the 1st Earl's time and has nothing to do with Hanoverian monarchs but is a reference to St. George, and the Order of the Garter and may commemorate either Lord Burghley's or the 1st Earl's installation as a Knight of the Garter, the highest Order of Chivalry in England. Elizabethan Burghley is principally due to the genius of Lord Burghley, but his son's architectural input should not be discounted. The 1st Earl commissioned John Thorpe (1565–*c.* 1655), then a clerk in the Office of Works to make surveys, which are inscribed to him, with plans to scale of the first and second floors of Burghley House in 1610. These are the best records of the Elizabethan house, showing the courtyard with flanking colonnades, the two-storeyed south front with an open loggia on the ground floor and state rooms above, the west front with the gatehouse and long gallery, and the family accommodation to the north, as well as the Great Hall and domestic offices in the east range. The latter survive, but all the other rooms were to be spectacularly remodelled and redecorated in the late seventeenth century, using some of the same artists and craftsmen used by the 5th Earl and Countess of Exeter. Those works were conducted on a scale and of a quantity to rival Charles II's reconstruction of the State Apartments at Windsor Castle in the 1660s and 1670s.

[19] The west elevation with central gatehouse and flanking towers of medieval inspiration.

[20] The west side of the courtyard

[21] The north side of the courtyard.

[22] *left & right*
The Roman Stairs, dating from 1560.

MORE IS MORE

[23] *left & right*
The west gatehouse vestibule, dated 1577.

[24] The fan-vaulted Kitchen. The immense painting of a butchered ox is by Frans Snyders (1579–1657). To the right is the Benham steam-warming cupboard, a nineteenth-century modernisation.

[25] The warm kitchen must have been a popular haven for staff to linger. The skulls are those of turtles, imported to make soup, perhaps placed by a chef to reinforce his Lordship's order.

It is expresly ordered by his
Lordship that no servants shall enter
the Kitchen except on business
or remain longer than is necessary
to perform what they have to do

[26] Chimneypiece in the Great Hall, dated 1575, after a design by Antonio Serlio.

[27] Detail of the chimneypiece with Lord Burghley's quartered arms.

DEO OPTIMO MAXIMO ET
MEMORIÆ SACRVM.
HONORATISSIM' & LONGE CLARISSIM' D GVILIELM' CECILI'
BARO: DE BVRGHLEY, SVMM' ANGLIÆ THESAVRARI' CVRIÆ PVPILLOR
PRÆFECT,' GEORGIANI ORDINIS EQVES AVRATVS, SERENISSIMÆ
ELIZABETHÆ ANGLIÆ & C. REGINÆ A SANCTIORIB' CONSILIIS,
& ACADEMIÆ CANTABRIGIENSIS CANCELLARI' SVB HOC TVMVLO
SECVNDVM CHRISTI ADVENTVM MANET.

[28] Lord Burghley's effigy on his tomb in St. Martin's Church, Stamford, dressed in armour and peer's robes, and holding the Lord Treasurer's wand of office.

[29] Lord Burghley's tomb of alabaster and coloured marble, bristling with obelisks and heraldry, erected after his death by the leading Southwark sculptor and Office of Works mason Cornelius Cure.

CHAPTER II

— The Stuart Religious and Cultural Vision —

THE ORIGINAL CREATION OF WILLIAM, Lord Burghley and his son Thomas, 1st Earl of Exeter survived undisturbed with little additional input from their immediate successors. This was partly due to the Civil War and Commonwealth in the 1640s and 1650s and the descent of the property and title to nephews or youngsters succeeding for relatively short periods, and little incentive for architectural improvement. Successive earls were traditionalist in religion and politics, and a love of rural life distanced them from metropolitan public affairs and spared the place from the impetus for change. The house was briefly besieged by the Parliamentarians in 1643 but little structural damage was done, though the south front is said to have been attacked by a light Cromwellian cannonade. A house like Burghley with its large mullion and transom windows was hardly a defensible structure, so fortunately avoided the 'slighting' which reduced more fortified places to ruins after capture by competing forces in the Civil War.

The 1st Earl was succeeded in 1622 by his only son William who presided at Burghley for eighteen years. Like his grandfather and namesake, he was educated at Cambridge (Trinity College in his case) and Gray's Inn. He was elected MP for Rutland and was appointed Lord Lieutenant of Northamptonshire for thirteen years, becoming a Knight of the Garter in 1630, the third of his family to be so honoured. According to the *Complete Peerage*, he converted to Catholicism as a young man but there is no evidence for the claim. His only son predeceased him, and he was succeeded as 3rd Earl by his nephew David who only held the title for three years before being succeeded in turn by his fifteen-year-old son John in the second year of the Civil War. In 1643 the conflict between King and Parliament came to Stamford and Burghley when Viscount Campden of Exton in Rutland occupied the town with a Royalist force, and then moved into Burghley House as Cromwell's forces approached. They did not hold out for long and the fact that the owner was a minor and his widowed mother still in charge must have protected the place from serious reprisals. The 4th Earl lived for eighteen years after the Restoration of the monarchy in 1660, dying in 1678, but he remains a shadowy figure. He married twice.

By his first marriage to Lady Frances Manners, daughter of the Earl of Rutland, the 4th Earl had a son, also John (1648–1700), whose succession ushered in the second major phase in the development of Burghley, and one which transformed the interior of the house and its contents with the addition of the most important collection in England of *Seicento* Italian paintings and the creation of rooms to display it. In this project the 5th Earl was supported by his wife Anne, the widow of Lord Rich. She was wealthy with strong views of her own and an active patron in her own right. She gave a strong religious tinge to the art collecting and was responsible for the rich upholstery which was a particularly strong ingredient of the new baroque interiors. Her fortune (from her first husband, and her mother) together with Lord Exeter's inheritances gave the impetus for the ambitious reconstruction which they undertook.

The role of the Exeters as lavish collectors and patrons is frequently misunderstood as an isolated precursor of the English Georgian Grand Tour, but it is better appreciated in the context of the seventeenth-century Stuart Court which had pursued a consistent Italophile cultural policy from Anne of Denmark (wife of James I), Henry Prince of Wales (who died young), King Charles I and his wife Henrietta Maria (daughter of Marie de Medici), through Charles II, and on to James II until the latter's dethronement in 1688.

In the course of his life the 5th Earl of Exeter made extensive visits to Italy on at least four occasions. His first tour, after succeeding was in 1679 and 1681, and he was accompanied by his wife Anne who came on his last travels too, though he revisited on his own in between. She shared all his cultural interests and her mark on the collection was

equally strong, especially as a result of a large inheritance of works of art from her mother, 'the Devonshire bequest'. Both were to some extent Catholic sympathisers, at least aesthetically, though Lord Exeter's epitaph on his tomb at Stamford stated that he 'supported the Protestant Faith', in case there might be doubt. The same was not claimed for his wife who judging from the contents of her personal apartments had stronger crypto-Catholic tastes than the earl. While the latter's love for Italian baroque art encompassed a large quantity of 'naked ladies' as recorded by Celia Fiennes on her visit in 1697 when she found 'fine painting in pictures, but they were all without Garments or very little that was the only fault, the immodesty of the Pictures, especially in my Lord's apartment.' Lady Exeter's pictures and objects were by contrast strikingly religious. They were not just Christian but Counter-Reformation, as demonstrated for instance in the works of Carlo Dolci in her Dressing Room and Closet, notably *Our Saviour blessing the Bread and Wine*, a celebration of the doctrine of transubstantiation which had been rejected by the Protestant sixteenth-century reformers but upheld by the Council of Trent and remains even today the most significant difference of dogma between Catholic and Protestant belief. This striking picture according to the 1738 inventory hung in Lady Exeter's Dressing Room adjoining her bedroom, with other religious items. It was an addition to the 1688 inventory being part of a later import from Italy, bought by the Exeters in Florence.

Anne Cavendish, Countess of Exeter was the daughter of the 3rd Earl of Devonshire while her mother Elizabeth was a Cecil of the Hatfield branch of the family being the daughter of the 2nd Earl of Salisbury. Anne's religious views may have been influenced by her mother whose nephew the 4th Earl of Salisbury converted to Catholicism in 1688. Her cultural interests derived from both her parents. The 3rd Earl of Devonshire had himself travelled to Italy when young with Thomas Hobbes as his tutor and had joined the philosopher in exile on the continent in 1642. He had strong classical and Italophile interests. Her mother was an avid collector who left all her rich possessions to Anne.

[30] *previous pages* Jean Tijou's splendid gilt wrought-iron gates are the centrepiece of the west front.

[31] *opposite left* Sir Peter Lely, *John Cecil, 5th Earl of Exeter*. Tory, collector and patron. He withdrew from Court after the fall and exile of James II, and perpetuated Stuart cultural policies at Burghley.

[32] *opposite right* Sir Peter Lely, *Anne, Countess of Exeter*. Sister of the 1st Duke of Devonshire and widow of Lord Rich. She shared her husband's artistic tastes and her inheritance and personal tastes were a strong element in the transformation of Burghley into a Baroque palace, notably the religious tinge of the picture collection.

[33] *below left* The Devonshire Schedule. The manuscript on vellum lists the possessions—including jewels, miniatures and precious objects—bequeathed by Elizabeth, Countess of Devonshire to her daughter Anne, Countess of Exeter, in 1690, with the proviso that they were for her personal possession, use and enjoyment, not her husband's.

[34] *below right* Carlo Dolci, *Christ Consecrating the Bread and Wine*. Bought by the 5th Earl in Florence in 1683. Lord Exeter was an enthusiast for Dolci's work which he knew through his friendship with Andrea del Rosso, a member of the Grand Duke's Court. Dolci's religiosity and meticulous technique appealed to Lord and Lady Exeter.

John, the 5th Earl of Exeter was a Tory and though not a Jacobite, a Stuart admirer. He shared the cultural vision of King Charles II and his brother James Duke of York who succeeded in 1685. James II only reigned for three years. He had been received into the Catholic Church as was publicly acknowledged in 1670, and he married as his second wife, Mary of Modena, an Italian princess in 1673. When he became king, Parliament was surprisingly not too hostile at first, partly because his religion was viewed as personal and a temporary blip, both James's daughters and heirs (by his first wife, Anne Hyde) being Protestant. James's autocratic attempts at ruling by Prerogative without Parliament soon made him unpopular. His hasty attempts to establish religious toleration were seen as an attack on the Church of England. He disturbed public and political feelings that had become embedded over the previous century. The birth of a son, James Francis Edward (the Old Pretender), in 1688 and the prospect of a permanent Catholic dynasty, on top of what the Whigs (the political successors of the mid-century Parliamentarians) saw as an autocratic undermining of the Constitution led to public opposition and rebellions. Princess Mary and her husband William of Orange were invited to take the throne. William landed in Devon and marched with his army to London. The Earl of Danby and his northern Whig supporters took York and Hull in William's name. James II fled into French exile, throwing the Great Seal—symbol of royal authority—into the River Thames as he left. He was deemed to have abdicated, and William and

[35] Benedetto Gennari, *Orpheus Playing his Music*. One of three paintings commissioned from Gennari in London in 1681 when he was Court Painter to Charles II and then James II. The artist followed King James into exile and returned to his native Bologna where he worked with his uncle Guercino. The 5th Earl dined with him there and commissioned more paintings from him in 1699.

Mary were invited by Parliament to take the throne in her father's place, and crowned as joint monarchs of England, France (the English claim to the French Crown was only given up in 1802), Ireland and Scotland.

The 5th Earl's sympathies remained with James II, and he refused to take the Oath of Allegiance to William III. He withdrew from public life and occupied himself with Continental travels, and collecting, building and gardening at Burghley which became the main point of his life. His Continental tours seem to have been carefully timed to avoid moments of political crisis like the Titus Oates Plot, the Glorious Revolution and the Battle of the Boyne which engulfed some of his friends. While staying out of public view, and not taking sides too obviously, he remained an admirer of Stuart cultural policies, which he spent his time perpetuating at Burghley House. It helped that his brother-in-law, with whom the Exeters remained on very friendly terms, had signed the encrypted letter inviting William III to take the throne and was created a duke as a result.

Lord Exeter had grown up against the backdrop of Charles II's cultural, as well as constitutional, revival. After the Restoration in 1660 Charles II had re-assembled as much as possible of his father's collection, and patronised Anthony Van Dyck's pupils and successors Peter Lely and Godfrey Kneller. While Charles I's Titians and other major paintings had been scattered irrevocably by Commonwealth sales all over Europe from Paris to Vienna, from Madrid to Bohemia, many of the later Italian paintings were retrieved and restored to Whitehall, St. James's, and other palaces. The king continued royal support for the Mortlake tapestry factory which had been founded by James I in 1619 and lavishly patronised by Charles I. He also built magnificent new state apartments at Whitehall Palace and especially at Windsor Castle where the Upper Ward was reconstructed by Hugh May, a gentleman architect, executed by a team specially gathered for the purpose including the Italian painter Antonio Verrio, the brilliant Flemish carver-sculptor Grinling Gibbons, and the Huguenot iron-worker Jean Tijou, and their English followers. Windsor established the English style for baroque interior decoration and was a key influence and object of emulation for the 5th Earl. He was inspired to create state rooms full of Italian art similar to those he knew at the Stuart Court, and this taste was reinforced by visits to France and Italy and especially the Pitti Palace in Florence and the Barbarini Palace in Rome where art was displayed in elaborately decorated state rooms, not in galleries.

Although overshadowed by the religious and constitutional debacle of his short reign, James II had continued the Stuart tradition as a royal patron of the arts. After the Restoration as Duke of York and heir apparent, he had his own apartments at St. James Palace which he decorated in baroque manner with tapestries and paintings and had his own chapel—still Anglican but 'High', described by Samuel Pepys as 'his pretty little chapel where I never was before, but silly devotions God knows'. For this James commissioned superb gold plate flagons, dishes, chalices—which is still an ornament of the Chapels Royal and some of which was used at Westminster Abbey for the coronation of King Charles III in May 2023. His bedroom had a magnificent gold brocade French bed made for the marriage to Mary of Modena.

On ascending the throne James II embarked immediately on architectural works at Whitehall to the design of Wren including new apartments for Queen Mary of Modena. The King's major architectural achievement at Whitehall, admired by Pepys despite his religious scruples, was a Catholic chapel with a towering angel-flanked marble altarpiece by the Antwerp sculptor Arnold Quellin (1653–1686). The altar paintings were in full-blown Italian style by the Bolognese Benedetto Gennari (1633–1715), the pupil and nephew of Guercino, who had worked for Charles II from

1674, and was re-appointed as Court painter by James. Other artists patronised by James II were the portrait painters Lely and Kneller, the Rome-trained Scottish Catholic John Michael Wright, and the painter of seascapes and naval engagements Willem van de Velde.

James's flight into exile aborted the King's cultural and religious policies. Gennari had to leave England and followed him to Saint-Germain-en-Laye in France before returning to his native Bologna where all his family worked in Guercino's workshop. The 5th Earl dined with him there in 1699 and commissioned three paintings from Gennari for Burghley, continuing Stuart artistic patronage. He had originally commissioned paintings from him when Gennari was in London, which are recorded in Gennari's *Account Book 1674–1688*: 'Questo per il sudetto Milord Exeter'. Many court artists and craftsmen moved directly from royal service to Burghley and the employ of the 5th Earl and Countess. Antonio Verrio had started to work at Burghley in 1686 but after the revolution in 1688 he refused to work for William III and moved with his family to Burghley and Stamford where he lived, and worked for Lord Exeter on and off for ten years, with intervals at Chatsworth painting for Lady Exeter's brother. Verrio was born and brought up in the Kingdom of the Two Sicilies and then worked in France before coming to England in 1672 at the invitation of Ralph, Duke of Montagu. His major work comprised twenty ceilings for Charles II in the state apartments at Windsor Castle (of which only three survive) as well as three

staircases, the Royal Chapel and St. George's Hall which was only completed in 1684, the year before Charles II died. At Burghley Verrio painted six ceilings and the whole of the Heaven Room, all of which survive. His talented assistant flower painter, Antonio Montignio, also added greatly to the overall impact, as in the naturalistic floral swags hanging in the trompe l'oeil colonnades of the Heaven Room walls. It is as if the Earl and Countess of Exeter were deliberately providing employment during their lifetimes for James II's artists. The creation of the new Burghley interiors was to all intents and purposes the continuation of Stuart work at Whitehall and Windsor.

The remodelling of Burghley began immediately after Lord Exeter inherited, a decade before the fall of James II. Work was in progress at the time of Lord Exeter's first visit to Italy to acquire works of art as an integral part of their programme for the house. His first visit, accompanied by Lady Exeter, coincided with Titus Oates Popish Plot when religious hysteria swept Britain between 1679 and 1681 and numerous people suspected of Catholic connections were accused of plotting to murder the King and Archbishop of Canterbury. The Exeter's friend Lord Arundell of Wardour was imprisoned in the Tower, and William Howard, Viscount Stafford was condemned to death for 'treason' on Oates's perjured evidence. Arundell and Stafford were both Italophile collectors and friends of Cosimo III Grand Duke of Tuscany (1642–1723) and patrons of the artist John Michael Wright.

The Exeters travelled in style, with their eldest son the five-year-old John, Lord Burghley, the house steward Culpepper Tanner, a chaplain and a large staff of nineteen servants as well as thirty horses, carriages and tents, cooking pots, soldiers, the family chaplain, and also their dog Towzer.

[36] Luca Giordano, *The Rape of Europa*. Bought by the 5th Earl in Florence (through his agent Mr. Balle) in 1683. Giordano visited Florence and was painting there in 1682, having been commissioned to decorate the Corsini Chapel in the Carmine. One of several works by the artist acquired directly in Florence by Lord Exeter.

[37] *below left* David de Koninck, *Hounds and Game*. Purchased in Rome by the 5th Earl in 1684. He had a particular liking for de Koninck's work. The spotted Dalmatian hound appears in several of de Koninck's paintings.

[38] *below right* Giuseppe Recco, *Still Life of Flowers in an Urn*. One of a pair acquired by the 5th Earl in Naples in 1684, and paid for through George Davies, the British Consul. Commissioned directly from the artist for 400 Ducats. They are the outstanding examples of Neapolitan flower painting in Britain.

In 1679 they spent the winter in Paris where they purchased furniture and tapestry at the Gobelins workshop, including the cabinet, table and guéridons by Pierre Gôle which had been made for Louis XIV but not taken by the King, before moving south via Tours and Lyons. They arrived in Genoa in November 1680. They then visited Padua, Venice, Lucca, Bologna, Florence and Rome where they spent Easter 1681.

On Lord Exeter's second visit in 1683 and 1684 he went on his own without his family or a large travelling household. This second tour was much more single-mindedly given over to the acquisition of art. In the winter of 1683 he stayed at the Court of Cosimo III where he commissioned many paintings from contemporary artists with the help of similarly art-minded Florentine courtiers, and his own agents—George Davies (Consul Naples), Thomas Hobson (Consul Venice), Robert and Thomas Balle (Florence).

He was presented by the anglophile Grand Duke with a pietra dura 'Cabinet Inlaid with stone and mother of perle' (to quote the 1688 Burghley Inventory). The inlaid marble panels representing birds, fruit and flowers were the work of the Grand Ducal workshop in the Galleria dei Lavori of the Uffizi and the cabinet work by Leonardo van der Vinne.

[39] Florentine pietra dura cabinet. Given to the 5th Earl by Cosimo III, Grand Duke of Tuscany, when Lord Exeter was in Florence in 1683. Of ebony inlaid with mother of pearl, and pietra dura panels, with gilt mounts, it is a masterpiece from the Grand Ducal workshops. It survives as the grandest piece of furniture at Burghley. The cabinet work with its superb marquetry is attributed to the Flemish cabinet-maker Leonardo van der Vinne who worked in Florence.

[40] Central pietra dura panel in the Florentine cabinet with a virtuoso display of a bowl of fruit, a bird and butterfly executed in coloured marbles, including lapis lazuli.

[41] Monument to the 5th Earl of Exeter and his wife Anne in St. Martin's Church, Stamford. It is by Pierre-Etienne Monnot, whom Lord and Lady Exeter met in Rome in 1700, while Monnot was working on the tomb of Cardinal Milvio in S. Maria del Popolo. They commissioned busts there of themselves, as well as this superb baroque marble tomb, Monnot's masterpiece.

Lord Exeter on his return placed it in pride of place in the family Drawing Room on the ground floor at Burghley; today it is prominent in the Fourth George Room and is the grandest piece of furniture in the house. In return Lord Exeter gave the Grand Duke an English carriage.

Through the agency of Mr. Balle in Florence he acquired two large canvases in 1683 of the *Rape of Europa* and the *Death of Seneca*, the work of the Neapolitan artist Luca Giordano who had been employed the previous year to paint the Corsini chapel in the church of the Carmine. They remain among the most impressive paintings at Burghley and now hang in the Third George Room. Giordano was greatly admired by Lord Exeter, and he went on to acquire thirteen works by the artist. His other great enthusiasm in Florence was for highly finished works of piety by Carlo Dolci, acquiring eight paintings by Dolci on this and future visits, partly with the advice of a Florentine Courtier del Rosso who had been the great patron of Dolci, and enthused Lord Exeter accordingly. Six paintings of devotional subjects by Dolci were hung by Lady Exeter in her private apartments when they arrived at Burghley.

Lord Exeter moved on to Rome from Florence in 1684, where he commissioned several pictures from Carlo Maratta for the large sum of 600 crowns. Maratta was then considered the greatest living Roman artist and was patronised by other English collectors including Sir Gyles Isham of Lamport, and the Earl of Sunderland of Althorp, both Northamptonshire neighbours. He also bought seven ever popular canvases of hounds and game by David de Koninck, another of the Earl's favourites, and four small paintings on copper by Filippo Lauri. In Rome he used as his art agent an English Catholic priest Fr. Bruno Talbot, cousin of the Earl of Shrewsbury.

From Rome he went on a twelve-day sightseeing trip to Naples where, as well as enjoying the ice creams, he commissioned two vast flower pieces from Giuseppe Recco for 400 ducats which he hung on his return in the Dressing Room of his private apartment at Burghley. Both are now in the Third George Room, or State Drawing Room, where they partner the two large Giordanos bought in Florence to make one of the most dazzling picture hangs in an English private house.

Further paintings were bought in the art centres of Bologna and Venice and finally in Genoa as he travelled north again. Forty-six paintings from Genoa including canvases by Tempesta and Assereto, were released to him by customs after it was confirmed 'that they were all bought by his Lordship himself for his own house at Burghley' which underlined the point of his Italian art-buying spree. His third shorter tour in 1693 was also devoted to art collecting.

Lord and Lady Exeter together embarked on the last of their Italian Grand Tours between 1699 and 1700. This time they took their two younger sons and daughter Elizabeth for their education. There was a more pronounced religious element on this occasion, and they went to Rome for the Holy Year of 1700 with visits to the seven major basilicas receiving a plenary indulgence. They also travelled to Loreto on the Aegean coast to see the Holy House, a major pilgrimage destination in Italy since the Middle Ages. On their way to Rome they dined en route with 'Mr. Gennari the painter' in Bologna on 8 December 1699. Lord Exeter had known him in London, and he now commissioned paintings from him in Italy. In Rome they lodged with John Dryden, Junior, the Catholic son of the English poet, and commissioned works including a marble bust, statues and their own tomb from Pierre-Etienne Monnot (1657–1733), the Roman-French sculptor who they met in Santa Maria del Popolo where Monnot was working on a bust for the tomb of Cardinal Savio Millini.

Lord Exeter was not just buying randomly. His art connoisseurship was informed, and all his collecting was undertaken with the eventual destination at Burghley in

H.S.E.
JOHANNES CECIL, Baro de Burghley, Exoniæ Comes, Magni Burley Abnepos haudquaquam degener. Egregiam enim
Indolem optimis Moribus optimis Artibus excoluit, Humanioribus literis bene instructus peregre plus vice Simplici
profectus est, et ab excultis Europæ regionibus multam Antiquitatum Linguarum nec non et rerum Civilium
scientiam reportavit. Cum Nemo forte melius vel Aulam ornare, vel curare Res Publicas posset, maluit tamen
Otium et Secessum Itaq. Ruri suo vixit eleganter, sumptuosè, splendidè, liberalibus Studijs oblectatus. Amicis comis
et jucundus. Egenis largus. Legum et Ecclesiæ ANGLICANÆ fortis semper Propugnator, suarum Virtutum et
Peregrinationum imo fere et scientiarum sociam habuit Uxorem ANNAM, ex prænobili domo de
CAVENDISH, GULIELMI Comitis Devoniæ Filiam, Corporis Formâ, et Animi Ingenio, et omnibus quæ
Fæminam decere possent, Dotibus insignem. E qua quinque Liberos suscepit. Fœlix Conjuge, fœlix et Prole
Sed inter omnia, vitam quæ faciunt beatiorem, Mortalitatis haud immemor, dum apud Italos præcipuæ Artis Opera
curiosus lustrabat, Hoc Monumentum illic, ubi exquisitissimè fieri potuit, Sibi et Charissimæ Lecti sui et Itinerum
et Curarum omnium Consorti.
Obijt Ille
F.F.
Obijt Illa

[42] Engraving of the south front of Burghley House, *c.* 1740. The 5th Earl enclosed the ground floor arcade and added the central Baroque doorcase designed by William Talman, Surveyor General to William III.

mind. For instance, the dimensions of overdoor height and space in the south dining room were especially measured for Pieter van Roestraten in 1681 when a still life was commissioned from him for that room. His tomb by Monnot in Stamford St. Martin shows him reclining in a toga with a pile of books by his side and he owned a significant library. He bought relevant publications during his travels to help with his collecting. In Rome in 1684, for instance, he acquired a copy of Raffaello Soprani, *Vite de' pittori scultori et architteti Genovesi* (1674), and used it in his buying of Genoese art. The forty-six paintings he acquired in Genoa at the end of his 1684 tour included the works of artists praised by Soprani in his book. His stays in the Court of the Medici in Florence, visit to Gennari in Guercino's studio in Bologna, or socialising with leading patrons, artists and sculptors like Monnot in Rome meant he could draw on local expertise when choosing artists. His contacts provided a knowledgeable base for his remarkable patronage of contemporary Italian art. In Florence, for instance, his friendships among the Grand Duke's courtiers who were themselves art connoisseurs included as has been seen Andrea del Rosso who had been one of Carlo Dolci's principal patrons and gave Lord Exeter Dolci's *Rest on the Flight into Egypt* and helped him buy other works by the artist. Lord and Lady Exeter's well-informed, even scholarly, collecting of paintings was motivated by the grand plan for the remodelling of Burghley House, of which the Italian art was a major, integral component.

The 5th Earl set about the reconstruction of the house as soon as he inherited. The exterior was left largely as Lord Burghley had created it but most of the interior was redecorated and palatially furnished. A skilled team was put together for the purpose, largely derived from the King's Works, just as Lord Burghley's had been a hundred years earlier. The architect chosen was William Talman (1650–1719), a protégé of the Earl of Clarendon, one of Charles II's ministers, for whom Talman designed Swallowfield Park in Berkshire. Clarendon like Exeter withdrew from Court following the deposition of James II but Talman had stayed on and been appointed Comptroller of Works by William III as successor to Charles II's architect the late Hugh May. Talman had an intransigent vexatious character and fell out with many of his clients in the course of his career, though there is no record of any quarrel with Lord Exeter who was drawn to the architect for his mastery of Italian baroque among a range of styles.

None of Talman's drawings for Burghley survive, but his involvement is otherwise documented. He is recorded as visiting in August and September 1688, and after Lord Exeter's death the executors paid Talman £200 owing in fees in 1704. This was a substantial sum and compares, for example, with the £40 Talman charged for visiting and drawing up unexecuted plans for the new house at Castle Howard in 1698, before he fell out with Lord Carlisle and was superseded by John Vanbrugh. Talman designed the south and east fronts, with the state rooms, at Chatsworth for Lord Exeter's brother-in-law, the first Duke of Devonshire from 1687 to 1696.

It is not clear if William Talman had visited Italy himself, but his son John stayed there on and off over twenty years and formed a large collection of objects and drawings and this rubbed off on his father. The Talmans and the Exeters therefore shared Italian cultural interests. William Talman understood Italian baroque architecture and his monumental south front at Chatsworth was inspired by Bernini's unexecuted design for the Louvre in Paris. His exterior work at Burghley, however, was restrained and respected Lord Burghley's Elizabethan masterpiece—no doubt following the directions of the client. The fenestration was regularised and leaded casements replaced with larger glass panes in sashes, a process completed by the 9th Earl in the later eighteenth century.

The principal external change was on the south front where the Elizabethan arcade on the ground floor was infilled with arched sash windows and a central baroque doorcase added with a dominant curved broken pediment enclosing an escutcheon of the arms of Cecil impaled with Cavendish. On the west front the central gateway was enclosed to make an entrance hall and the archway filled with magnificent wrought iron gates by Tijou, gilded to splendid effect by René Cousin. As part of these external improvements, the Earl and Countess created a suitable baroque garden setting. Between 1678 and 1685 the 5th Earl spent £450 on the purchase of trees, representing about 5,000 specimens. In 1683 the Royal gardener George London drew up plans for formal gardens with topiary, fountains, pools, sculpture, and radiating avenues. In the 1690s London laid out a formal parterre before the south front with a big central fountain; beyond it the mile-long Queen Anne's Avenue was planted in 1702, the year before the Countess died. London was paid his last bill amounting to £254 in 1704.

Celia Fiennes on her visit in 1697 was struck: 'the gardens very fine within one another with lower and higher walls with Statues and fine grass walks, dwarfs and all sort of green trees and curious things, very fine fountains, there is one in the middle [on axis] of the house that is of exceeding great size'. This explains the grand baroque doorcase on the south front which was the backdrop centrepiece to all this. Apart from Queen Anne's Avenue, none of the 5th Earl's and London's layout survived the even more ambitious transformation of the setting by Capability Brown for the 9th Earl.

[43] Gilded wrought-iron gates on the north entrance, by the French Huguenot smith, Jean Tijou. Celia Fiennes, the traveller, thought them the finest extant ironwork.

Within the house the 5th Earl and Countess's work was much more sweeping, amounting to an almost total reconstruction. Only the Great Hall, Kitchen and Roman Stair on the east side remained untouched, possibly because the Great Hall was not used much, except as a storeroom with the fire engine parked there. The south, west and north ranges, however, were totally remodelled on all floors. The work in the south range created new rooms with the enclosure of the ground floor arcade, and the re-planning of the George Rooms on the main floor, possibly making good damage on this side from the Cromwellian cannonade. The 1690s re-planning of the state rooms is shown by comparing John Thorpe's survey of 1610 with the larger Presence Chamber occupying the site of the present Heaven Room and Fourth George Room and two further rooms of lesser dimensions. The 5th Earl rearranged to create a Great Room, Dining Room, Drawing Room and State Bedroom, with the State Dressing Room occupying the south end of the west wing. Whereas the Elizabethan house had three or four royal rooms, the 5th Earl created an up-to-date enfilade of five rooms with the insertion of a drawing room which was a Stuart innovation pioneered by Charles I in his palaces. The Dressing Room in the west range followed the subdivision of the Elizabethan Long Gallery there.

The work in the west range created two apartments for Lord and Lady Exeter on the ground floor symmetrically arranged on either side of the West Hall, a similar arrangement for important guests was contained on the first floor by subdividing the Long Gallery, and seven simpler bedrooms on the top floor in place of the Upper Gallery. On the north side the piano nobile was grandly remodelled to create rooms for public entertaining.

Culpepper Tanner, the House Steward, who was the Exeter's right hand man in all the works, and managed the finances, drew up an inventory in 1688, the year of the deposition of James II. It shows that the new ground floor apartments for Lord and Lady Exeter were complete, but the main George Rooms were not yet begun.[4] The inventory records the furniture commissioned in England from leading London cabinet makers and upholsterers including seven 'imperial beds' from the Huguenots Francis Lapierre II and Pierre Dufresnoy, similar to the Chatsworth bed (now in the Gallery at Hardwick) by Lapierre, or James II's French silver and gold bed (now in the King's Bedroom at Knole). Such masterpieces of elaborate upholstery were the most expensive items of Stuart furniture. In addition there were numerous sets of chairs by the London craftsman Robert Cookman and luxury furniture by the Royal cabinet maker Gerreit Jensen in Franco-Dutch taste.

The new rooms created in the 1680s on the ground and first floors of the west range have a uniform architectural character with well-made oak joinery and wainscot by Roger Davis, the doyen of his trade who was employed at Burghley for several years from 1678 onwards. The bolection moulded marble chimneypieces were centred in some rooms or took the fashionable form of corner fireplaces

[44] The 1688 Inventory of Burghley House, compiled by the House Steward, Culpepper Tanner, and recording many of the works of art acquired in Paris and Italy, and the new furnishings of the ground floor west rooms created for Lord and Lady Exeter's personal occupation in the 1680s.

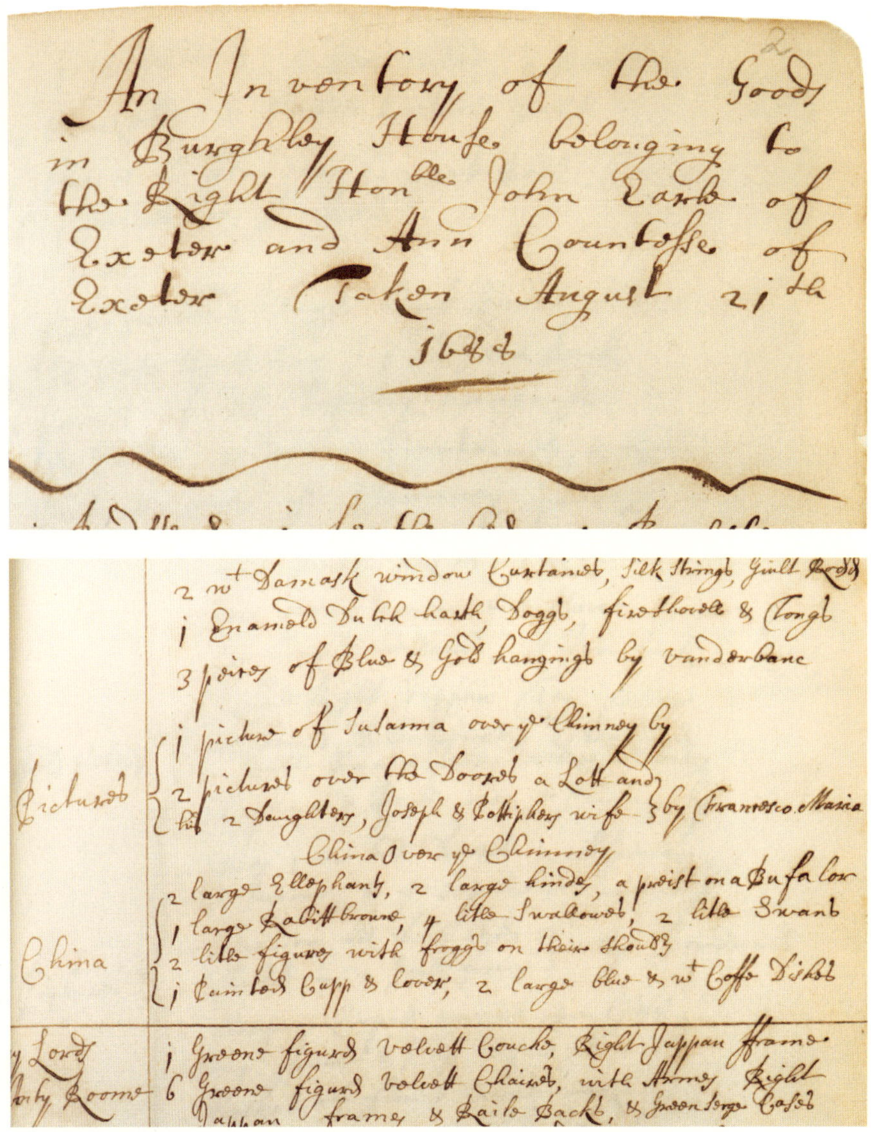
An Inventory of the Goods in Burghley House belonging to the Right Hon.ble John Earle of Exeter and Ann Countesse of Exeter Taken August 21th 1688

2 wt Damask window Curtaines, Silk Strings, Guilt Rods
1 Enameld Dutch hearth Doggs, fireshovell & Tongs
3 peires of Blue & Gold hangings by Vanderbanc
Pictures
1 picture of Salama over ye Chimney by
2 pictures over the Doores a Lott and his 2 daughters, Joseph & Pottiphers wife 3 by Francesco Maria
China over ye Chimney
China
2 large Ellophants, 2 large hindes, a priest on a Bufalow
1 large Rabitt Browne, 4 litle Swallowes, 2 litle Swans
2 litle figures with froggs on their shoulds
1 painted Cupp & Cover, 2 large blue & wt Coffe Dishes
My Lords Anty Roome
1 Greene figured velvett Couch, Right Jappan frame
6 Greene figured velvett Chaires, with Armes, Right Jappan frames & Raile backs, & greene serge Cases

with tiers above for the display of imported Oriental—Japanese and Chinese—porcelain of which the 5th Earl and Countess's collection is the earliest to be identifiably documented in England. The more important rooms had carved overmantels, overdoors and cornices in the manner of Grinling Gibbons, and deeply moulded stucco ceilings of different patterns of geometrical panels and hand modelled fruit, flowers and foliage. This plasterwork and the wood carving are spectacular achievements by a group of London craftsmen, notably Edward Marten the stuccoist, and Jonathan Mayne (or Maine) and Thomas Young, woodcarvers who went on to work at Chatsworth for the Duke of Devonshire, Lady Exeter's brother. The prominence of plaster ceilings at Burghley differentiates it from the parallel baroque transformation at Chatsworth.

Lord and Lady Exeter's ground floor apartments were planned *en enfilade* on either side of the West Hall and were constructed while the occupants were away in 1679 and 1681, though furnished under their joint direction after their return in 1682. Another reason for the Exeter's regular visits to the Continent, in addition to political expediency, religion, education and sightseeing, and collecting art, was to avoid the upheavals in the house while the interior reconstruction was in progress. Tanner's 1688 inventory describes the interiors when first completed with the art collected on the tours of 1679 and 1683, though their contents continued to be enriched with the acquisitions from further tours. During their travels Lord and Lady Exeter bought tapestries, furniture and many pictures described in situ in the inventory, but much continued to arrive and an MS addition records 'Several Pictures bought and brought into Burghley House since the foregoing Inventory'.

Lord Exeter's apartment lay to the north of the West Hall. His Ante Room was panelled in oak, with green figured velvet upholstery and white damask curtains, and japanned furniture in the height of London fashion (that is, painted to resemble lacquer). It contained seven paintings of Venuses, Judgments of Paris and the like; three similar in the adjoining bedroom, shocked Celia Fiennes in 1697. Lord Exeter's bedroom was hung with tapestries of Venus and Cupid by John Vanderbank of the Soho Tapestry Factory, which still hang there. The Dressing Room beyond had blue damask chairs and curtains and contained among other paintings, the two large flower pieces by Giuseppe Recco commissioned in Naples in 1684. They were later moved to the more appropriately scaled George Rooms. To the north there was access to the library containing Lord Exeter's art and architecture books in a projecting wing (demolished in the eighteenth century), and there was a second dressing room in the north range called the Tiled Room.

Lady Exeter's apartment formed a mirror image to the south of the West Hall and was even more richly decorated and furnished. Her 'Anty Roome' was panelled in oak with white damask curtains, and thirteen paintings on the walls. Over the chimneypiece was displayed an English medieval alabaster Pietà, the *Virgin with the Body of Our Saviour*,

[45] Gobelins Tapestry, commissioned by Lord and Lady Exeter directly from the workshop in the early 1680s for the remodelled rooms. It depicts Bacchus crowning Ariadne, with a shell border and the arms of Cecil impaled with Cavendish.

[46] English fifteenth-century alabaster Pieta. This very rare English medieval survival was recorded in 'My Lady's Anty Room' in 1688, one of many religious works of art displayed in Lady Exeter's apartments.

of the type that had been destroyed in their thousands by the Reformation iconoclasts. This was a very unusual object to find in an English late seventeenth-century art collection and underlined the religious dimension of Lady Exeter's taste. The paintings were similarly religious and included Francesco Trevisani's *Noli me Tangere* and Giuseppe Bartolomeo Chiari's *Virgin and Magdalene mourning the dead Christ*. Lady Exeter's Bed Chamber was hung with the five Jan Jans Gobelins tapestries of the *Fables of La Fontaine* which had been ordered in Paris at the beginning of the first Grand Tour in 1679, presumably with this location in mind. The imperial bed was hung with blue silk damask and the chairs covered to match. The furniture included a set of japanned tables and matching gueridons or candle stands. The Dressing Room was hung with crimson damask and Indian flowered silk, and seven paintings mainly with a religious tone which included Luca Giordano's *Woman Taken in Adultery*. Over the chimneypiece were arranged many pieces of Oriental porcelain, exotics like '2 Cocus Nutt shells' and carved boxwood figures of Cleopatra and Pallas, part of a group of eight bought for sixty crowns in Italy which remain at Burghley. The Closet was hung with green figured velvet and massed ranks of forty paintings including six devotional works by Carlo Dolci and many miniatures. Two more of the boxwood figures were displayed in here. The most striking feature was the luxurious floor of floral marquetry. (This was later taken up for practical reasons, but the marquetry was saved.) Some of the objects as well as the paintings had a religious significance such as the 'silver sprigs of flowers' over the chimneypiece, part of a set made in Milan. These were silver altar ornaments.

The 1688 inventory describes Lady Exeter's rooms before the massive augmentation of her possessions by inheritance from her mother the Countess of Devonshire who died in

[47] *below left* Carved boxwood figure of Pallas Athene, one of a set of eight bought by Lord and Lady Exeter in Italy for 60 crowns. It was in Lady Exeter's Dressing Room in the 1688 Inventory.

[48] *below right* Italian silver flowers, one of several from Milan. They were made in Italy as altar ornaments. In the 1688 Inventory, two vases of 'silver flower spriggs' were in Lady Exeter's closet which had something of the character of a private oratory.

1689 leaving her £32,000. This included all the contents of Lady Devonshire's apartment at Chatsworth and fixtures like the marble windowsills, a silver lock, curtains and tapestries as well as sixty-four oil paintings, many miniatures and watercolours, porcelain, and a *Schatzkammer* of sixteenth- and seventeenth-century jewels, rock crystal vessels, silver and gold work. Such a surviving assemblage is unique in an English country house. The bequest which must have transformed the Countess's apartment at Burghley came with the proviso that these heirlooms were 'For [her] peculiar use and benefit and at [her] disposal . . . with which the . . . Earl of Exeter should not intermeddle and nor should the same in any sort by lyable to his debts Arts or Disposition'.[5] This was an interesting comment on Lady Exeter's independence as a collector and patron in her own right, and she herself took an active part in the Grand Tours.

The new rooms in the enclosed arcade on the south front were family rooms finished in the same style as the Exeters' apartments. They comprised the 'Best Bedd Chamber' hung with another set of Jan Jans Gobelins tapestries from

Sir. G. Kneller
78

80

opposite page, clockwise from top left

[49] The Devonshire 'Schatzkammer' bequeathed to Lady Exeter by her mother, the wife of the 3rd Earl of Devonshire, from Chatsworth.

[50] Sir Godfrey Kneller, *Self Portrait*. One of a group of ovals depicting the members of the 5th Earl's private drinking club 'The Honourable Order of Little Bedlam', established at Burghley in 1684. Each member had an animal avatar included in their portrait. Kneller's was a unicorn.

[51] Sir Godfrey Kneller, *Portrait of Antonio Verrio*, who spent a decade at Burghley painting the ceilings of the staterooms. His club avatar, just visible bottom left, was a porcupine.

[52] Gold and enamelled jewels forming part of the Devonshire 'Schatzkammer'.

[53] Silver lock from Lady Devonshire's apartment at Chatsworth, bequeathed to her daughter in 1690.

this page

[54] Examples from the collection of Japanese porcelain acquired by the 5th Earl and Countess. They are listed in the 1688 Inventory, making them the earliest documented Japanese porcelain in Europe. The pair of Arita tankards were described as 'brown Juggs, over the chimneypiece in the drawing room'. The large elephants, a pair, were in 'My Lord's Bedd Chamber' in 1688. The Wrestling boys, in iron-red fushima loin cloths, were in the 'Wardrobe or Clock Tower' in 1688. The Arita puppies are a pair of charming 'Dogges'. Lord Exeter was a characteristic English dog-lover.

[55] *opposite* Pair of very rare English mid-seventeenth-century porcelaneous vases and covers. Of soft paste, copying the Chinese guan form, it is thought these were made in the short-lived Lambeth factory established by George Villiers, 2nd Duke of Buckingham at the Restoration. They were part of the Devonshire bequest to Anne, Countess of Exeter.

Paris, depicting Ovid's Metamorphoses, and containing an Imperial bedstead upholstered in crimson damask. This room next to her own apartment was intended for Lady Exeter's Devonshire relations on their journeys between London and Chatsworth. The furniture included a cabinet of Japanese export lacquer inlaid with mother-of-pearl on an English carved and gilt stand, which is still in the collection. Over the chimneypiece were displayed the other four boxwood figures depicting Alexander, Mars, Cicero and Catalina, and twenty-one pieces of porcelain. Beyond was the 'Drawing Roome' hung with blue velvet, where the Grand Duke's pietra dura cabinet took pride of place, and several of the Italian paintings were displayed, including the two large Giordanos bought in 1683. In the centre, giving access to the garden, was the 'Salloon Roome' or Marble Hall, so called from the sculpture displayed there, and with family portraits including the 5th Earl and Countess by Lely framed into the oak wainscot. The carved overmantel and Marten's stucco ceiling are the finest on the ground floor. East of the Marble Hall was the dining room hung with crimson figured velvet and with sixteen chairs upholstered to match. The four large paintings on the walls included two by Johan Carl Loth bought in Venice in 1684. Beyond was the Tea Room which no longer exists, with access from the Great Stairs.

The inner east range contained a central hall (giving access to the Great Hall). It was decorated in the 1690s by Alexander Souville, Verrio's 'architecture' assistant, as was the West Hall, but both of Souville's schemes have disappeared. The East Hall was flanked by the 'Guilt Leather Dining Roome' and the 'Smoaking Roome'. This area was dedicated to jolly masculine revels, far from the family apartments. It was used by Lord Exeter's private drinking club the 'Honourable Order of Little Bedlam' for friends and artists. Both Kneller and Verrio were members as well as brother-in-law Devonshire, the Dean of Windsor, and the poet and scholar Matthew Prior (1664–1721) who acted for a time as tutor to Lord Exeter's eldest son. Prior's easy, charming, satiric humour was just the sort to appeal to Lord Exeter. Each member of the Bedlam Club was identified by an animal and their eponymous animal was included in the corners of their club portraits. Verrio's was a porcupine. These rooms were furnished with 'Spanish' folding tables made by Roger Davis, the wainscot joiner who probably was responsible for much of the new frame furniture, as opposed to the upholstered, exotic and Grand Tour items. The chairs were upholstered in 'Spanish Leather'.

The first floor continued to be state rooms, as in the Elizabethan house. The remodelling of the north and west ranges was under way by 1688 and served *pro tem* as the principal entertaining rooms. The grandest was the central north Bow Room, twenty-five feet high, which served as a dining room, continuing its likely Elizabethan purpose. It was only decorated in 1697, not by Verrio who left that year to return to Royal service and paint the staircase at Hampton Court. It was done by his colleague from Chatsworth, Louis Laguerre (a godson of Louis XIV). Laguerre signed and dated his work on the wall opposite the fireplace. His decoration covers the whole of the walls and ceiling, with much trompe architecture in the form of coffering, 'marble' columns, and pilasters decorated with ribbons, leaves and fruit, paralleling Laguerre's schemes in the Hall and Chapel at Chatsworth. The paintings are devoted to Roman history: Antony and Cleopatra, the Continence of Scipio, the Battle of Philippi. Laguerre's palate is darker than Verrio's, closer to Charles Lebrun at Versailles. The white marble chimneypiece incorporates three expensive panels of looking glass. It is the most elaborate of the seventeenth-century fireplaces and also parallels work at Chatsworth.

To the west were the Drawing Room, State Bedroom, and its Dressing Room completed by 1688. They shared

the same architectural treatment as the ground floor, the work of the same craftsmen but richer and grander. There is oak panelled wainscot by Davis, deeply moulded stucco ceilings by Marten, and elaborate carved overmantels and overdoors by Maine and Young. The North Drawing Room (now Brown Drawing Room) was hung with English Mortlake tapestries of Psyche, and contained the cabinet, table and gueridons by Pierre Gôle bought by the Exeters at the Gobelins in 1679. The adjoining State Bedroom called by Tanner 'The Bed Chamber next ye Gallery Roomes' was hung with Mortlake tapestries from the *Playing Boys* series and had a new 'Imperial Bedstead' and chairs to match with gilt and painted frames supplied by Daniel Cookman of London circa 1680. (Part of the set survives in the house.) There was also a smaller ebony and pietra dura Florentine cabinet acquired circa 1682. Cookman provided much of the smart new seat-furniture, and substantial payments to him are recorded in Lord Exeter's account at Child's Bank between 1678 and 1683. Banks and the finance they provided were a new development in the late seventeenth century, and Sir Francis Child (1642–1713) was important in underpinning and enabling Lord Exeter's extravagant patronage. Francis Child was the first London goldsmith to become a professional banker in the modern sense and his funding of Lord Exeter's building and collecting was a new capitalist development at the time. He and the Duke of Devonshire became Lord Exeter's trustees.

The 'Gallery Roomes' formed out of Lord Burghley's Long Gallery in the 1680s repeated the layout on the ground floor, with two apartments to the north and south of a central Saloon (now the Pagoda Room) which itself displayed two of the large paintings by David de Koninck bought in Rome in 1684. The guest bedrooms, too, were hung with tapestries and furnished with imperial bedsteads hung with scarlet mohair and green and white hangings. Upholstery and textiles played a large role in the impact of the interior. Payments of £1,200 are recorded to the upholsterers Dufresnoy and Lapierre. Lady Exeter supervised much of this aspect of the decorations. The smaller dressing rooms had corner chimneypieces and were part hung with blue and crimson damask. The joinery around the doors and chimneypieces and dadoes was 'grained' or painted to resemble coloured marble and this extended to the tiered overmantels for porcelain, like stepped pyramids, over the chimneypiece, a decorative treatment recently restored.

The most ambitious part of the remodelling was the enfilade of state rooms, forming a palatial apartment on the piano nobile of the south front. These were twenty-four feet high as they rose to the roof with no second floor above them. They marked a notable increase in scale from the 'Gallerye Rooms' in the west range which were only sixteen feet high. They are comparable with Charles II's state rooms at Windsor and the Duke of Devonshire's at Chatsworth, created by the same team of craftsmen and artists, and considerably grander than the state rooms at Boughton. The principal feature of the George Rooms is the sequence of painted ceilings which forms the most extensive surviving work by Verrio. His employment is recorded in over 300 surviving letters and accounts. He was paid his first instalment of £50 in 1686 towards the ceilings of the State Dressing Room or First George Room, and its adjoining closet. Verrio and his team of assistants worked consecutively through the rooms from west to east finishing with the ceiling over the 'Great Stairs' (now called the Hell Staircase from the subject of his painting), completed in 1697, after which Verrio left Burghley and belatedly returned to Royal service, after his long sojourn with the Exeters and Devonshires. The subjects were, as to be expected, classical mythology. The First George Room ceiling depicted 'Morning Chasing Night' and the adjoining Jewel Closet 'Fortune Blind-Folded'. The Second George Room (the bedroom) celebrated the 'Rewarding of Virtue'. The Third George Room (the drawing room) was devoted to the Reconciliation of Cupid and Psyche. The Fourth George Room (the dining room) had on the ceiling a 'Feast of the Gods'. The Fifth George Room (the Heaven Room) had walls and ceiling with 'An Assembly of the Gods' in a strongly architectural setting. The staircase ceiling showed a classical 'Hell' and made a dramatic climax to the series.

Verrio was employed by contract, a shrewd business move no doubt with the advice of the House Steward, Culpepper Tanner. He was a 'difficult' character fully imbued with Italian artistic temperament, often drunk, a gourmand and jolly libertine with a family of two dissolute sons. On one occasion the generally easy-going Lord Exeter called him an 'impudent dogg', but generally the artist was cosseted. The household accounts include culinary treats and plenty to drink. In one year he was supplied with '12 of claret, 6 of Canary [a sweet wine], 2 of port, ½ pint of brandy' as well as special delicacies like '*saucissons de Boulogne*'. Lord Exeter got the best out of him with a combination of a strict enforceable business arrangement, overseen by the astute Culpepper and pampering: stick and carrot.

Under the terms of his contract, Verrio paid for all his materials and the wages of his mainly Huguenot assistants who included René Cousin, the gilder, and Alexander Souville, the architecture-painter, as well as lesser helpers. Cousin was also generally employed at Burghley for all the gilding including Tijou's dazzling west gate screen. Souville's architecture-painting was of high quality. The Huguenot craftsmen who came to England from France after the repeal of the Edict of Nantes in 1685, as well as metal workers like Tijou, silk weavers and upholsterers like Lapierre, also included a group of decorative painters like James Parmentier, Louis Chéron (who worked at Chatsworth and Boughton but not at Burghley) and Souville. Little is known of Souville but he was still working in London in 1713. His architecture-painting at Burghley is his only surviving documented work and comprises the trompe decoration of the coves of the first four George Rooms and the spectacular Corinthian arcades and convincingly stepped plinth of the Heaven Room, and the heroically scaled bracket cornice of the Great Stairs. Lord Exeter was employing Huguenots as soon as they came to England, another mark of his up-to-date patronage.

Verrio's work is often denigrated by modern critics, including Nikolaus Pevsner, as lacking brio and being inferior to Italian contemporaries at home. In fact his work can hold its own with much late seventeenth-century decorative painting in France or Italy. His colours are good, especially his blues which dazzle in the tented canopy over

[56] French cabinet and stand by Pierre Gôle, 1675, bought directly from the Gobelins factory in Paris by the 5th Earl and Countess on their visit in 1683. It is probable that it was made originally for Louis XIV for the Château of Vincennes, and Lord Exeter was able to acquire it when the King changed his mind. This masterpiece of French cabinetmaking is one of the earliest examples of French floral marquetry and the finest of its type to survive.

Venus in bed with Mars on the west wall of the Heaven Room, or delicious late-Mannerist shades of pink and lemon in the ceilings. His compositions can rise to striking drama as in the Hell ceiling. He regarded himself as a specialist in figure painting, those skills being demonstrated in the over-life-size gods and goddesses bursting through the encircling columns of the Heaven Room. The one-eyed Cyclops working in Vulcan's forge or Verrio's own adjoining self-portrait are striking images. His classical themes are also enlivened by considerable humour.

Much of the lukewarm criticism from Pevsner and followers dates from before the cleaning of the ceilings and murals in the 1990s, which transformed their impact, revealing the range of flesh tones, Italian colours, and the liveliness of the figures and portraits. Apart from their artistic merit, Verrio's paintings capture some of the fun of the 5th Earl's easy-going *train-de-vie* at late seventeenth-century Burghley with its Little Bedlam drinking club. They incorporate satirical portraits of friends in classical garb: the Dean of Windsor is portrayed as drunken Bacchus, Lord Exeter's sons are mischievous winged putti climbing a Corinthian column, and the cook is shown as 'Plenty', naked with six breasts. Such allusions would have been as obvious to contemporary onlookers as the identities of the Greek and Roman gods. The visual jokes enlivened the ostensibly classical mythologies, a combination of the junketings of Lord Exeter and his friends and their classical learning.

The 1690s George Rooms formed an enfilade of five rooms just as at Chatsworth and Boughton. Their proportions were graded sequentially from the Heaven Room which was thirty-nine feet long, through the Dining Room which was thirty-one feet, the Drawing Room twenty-seven feet square, the State Bedroom twenty-three feet and the Dressing Room the smallest. (Though the ceremonial sequence works from Heaven to Dressing, the George Rooms have always been numbered from the opposite end.) The heightened architectural tone was not just their proportions and the painted ceilings, but their intended wall and floor treatments, with more elaborate carving, gilding, and floors of *parquet de Versailles*. In the event only the First George Room, the State Dressing Room and its cedar-lined closet were finished in Lord Exeter's lifetime. It gives a clear indication of the intention for the whole. The carved acanthus leaf cornice there is gilded. The mouldings of the oak wainscot are enriched with classical detail, unlike the 'Gallerye Roomes' which have plain mouldings. The three carved entablatures of the overdoors are the finest in the house and the best candidates for being autograph work by Grinling Gibbons. He was paid £50 in 1683 and £50 in 1685 without specifying for what, but these trophies 'fit the bill'. They are not just swags, flowers and game birds but have Gibbons's hallmarks like musical instruments, arrows, beads and medals. Gibbons always

[57] Overdoor in the First George Room, the state dressing room, by Grinling Gibbons. The three carved limewood overdoors in the dressing room are the only work by the doyen of seventeenth-century wood carvers at Burghley, who was paid 100 pounds for this work. The fine oak and lime carvings in similar style elsewhere in the house were by the London team of Thomas Young and Jonathan Maine. The Gibbons trophy includes arrows, musical instruments and Lord Exeter's cypher and coronet.

worked in limewood while his English followers often stuck to oak as in Jonathan Maine's fluent and sophisticated overmantel downstairs in the Marble Hall, which is a wonder in its own right, if not as virtuoso as Gibbons.[6]

The 5th Earl died suddenly in Paris in 1700 on the return from the Exeters' last tour. His widow lived for three more years, overseeing the last influx of Italian paintings. She erected the tomb, which they had presciently commissioned from Monnot in Rome, near Lord Burghley's at St. Martin's church. Lord Exeter had spent extravagantly, though unlike his ancestor he held no Court offices or lucrative public employments. His income came entirely from his estates and his and his wife's inheritances, and all were exhausted by the time of their deaths, leaving the 6th Earl and successors with large debts of over £38,000 which took years to clear. The George Rooms were left incomplete without wall coverings, chimneypieces or floorboards. In 1697 Celia Fiennes noted 'some floors not laid'. George Vertue some years after the Exeters' deaths found 'all in sad disorder and the floors unfinished as left by the Earl who was a great collector and lover of art'. As late as 1785 the rooms were still 'unfinished',[7] but by then the 9th Earl had embarked on their completion in the spirit of his predecessor's baroque intentions, and it is due to him that the enfilade of State Rooms was finally finished and furnished as the most magnificent in England; described by Christopher Hussey in the 1950s as 'unmatched even at Windsor or Hampton Court'.

[58] Looking from the Jewel Closet to the First George Room.

[59] Detail of Tijou's wrought-iron gates on the north entrance.

[60] Looking out through the west arch and the Tijou gates. The glazing was added in the nineteenth century.

[61] The Red Drawing Room in the ground floor family apartments, with the rich stucco ceiling by Edward Marten, a key figure of the Exeters' team of first-rate craftsmen. It is one of a large series along the south and west fronts. The huge overmantel mirror was made by Mayhew and Ince for the 9th Earl.

[62] *left & right*
Enfilade from the Marble Hall through the south front ground floor rooms. They have slightly simpler oak joinery than the state rooms upstairs, and stucco rather than painted ceilings. The carved marble figure of the seated Mercury is early nineteenth century, after Thorvaldsen.

[63] The former dining room, now a drawing room, on the ground floor, with Marten's fine stucco ceiling and carved limewood swag overmantel by Young and Maine. The marble chimneypiece and sideboard alcove with Corinthian columns were inserted by the 9th Earl.

[64] The 9th Earl's Dressing Room on the ground floor, with a moulded stucco ceiling by Edward Marten and tapestry on the walls.

[65] The Dressing Room of Anne Countess of Exeter, now a principal guest bedroom, with moulded stucco ceiling by Marten and a superb carved stained limewood overmantel by Young and Maine—their masterpiece.

[66] *left & right*
Lord Exeter's bedroom with stucco ceiling, carved overmantel, Vanderbank tapestries and the 'imperial' bed, remodelled by Mayhew and Ince for the 9th Earl but retaining a baroque character.

SPQR

[67] The Bow Room in the centre of the north first floor, with murals by Louis Laguerre (the godson of Louis XIV). The large scene depicts the Continence of Scipio. This room was intended as the 5th Earl's state dining room.

[68] The Bow Room with Talman's seventeenth-century marble chimneypiece and the Laguerre mural depicting Anthony and Cleopatra in a *trompe l'oeil* baroque frame.

[69] English Soho tapestries with arabesques in the Black and Yellow Bedroom. It was the State bedroom in the 5th Earl's time.

[70] Interior of the seventeenth-century bed in the Black and Yellow Bedroom, with restored needlework hangings.

[71] The Black and Yellow Bedroom showing the seventeenth-century bolection moulded chimneypiece and carved overmantel by Young and Maine.

[72] The Marquetry Room. The series of five rooms along the west side of the house was made by subdividing the Long Gallery.

[73] A glimpse of Queen Elizabeth's Bedroom in the western enfilade.

206
552
121

[74] *left & right*
Detail of the restored blue silk hangings on the seventeenth-century bed attributed to Lapierre in Queen Elizabeth's Bedroom. (Queen Elizabeth, of course, never slept in it.)

[75] Engraved seventeenth-century brass lock on the doors of the new baroque rooms.

[76] The Pagoda Room. The central ante room between the two grand suites of guest bed- and dressing-rooms created by the 5th Earl out of Lord Burghley's Long Gallery. (Its present name derives from the eighteenth-century Chinese model pagoda displayed here.)

[77] Carved oak door architraves in the George Rooms, which compose the south enfilade on the *piano nobile*.

[78] Detail of the Soho tapestry by John Vanderbank in the Second George Room, incorporating depictions of Burghley House in the borders. Commissioned by the 5th Earl and his Countess.

[79] The Blue Silk Bedroom with the 'imperial bed' as remodelled by Mayhew and Ince. The Gôle cabinet made at the Gobelins factory takes pride of place here.

[80] Detail of the floral marquetry on the drawers of the Gôle cabinet in the Blue Silk Bedroom.

[81] The Blue Silk Dressing Room. The marbled decoration and porcelain display on the tiered corner chimneypiece have been restored according to the description in the 1738 Inventory.

237
232
269
52
59
500a

[82] The Jewel Closet in the southwest corner of the *piano nobile*, the smallest of the state rooms which have always been known as the George Rooms, after the Order of the Garter.

[83] The First George Room with Verrio's painted ceiling depicting Morning Chasing Night. It was the only one of the George Rooms, apart from the Jewel Closet, to be completed in the 5th Earl's lifetime, with superlative carved oak joinery and a floor of parquet de Versailles, and was intended to be the state dressing room.

[84] The Fourth George Room, the state dining room, with Verrio's ceiling depicting a Feast of the Gods. The oak wainscot and carved and gilt cornice were completed by the 9th Earl as had originally been intended. The walls are hung with the 5th Earl's best Italian *seicento* pictures, and the Grand Duke of Tuscany's pietra dura cabinet is in pride of place.

[85] Detail of the Grand Duke's cabinet, with pietra dura panels.

[86] The Heaven Room, or Fifth George Room. The first in the ceremonial sequence and grandest of the Baroque state apartments, replacing Lord Burghley's Great Chamber. It was entirely painted by Antonio Verrio and his assistants with mythological scenes in a *trompe* architectural setting. The latter was by Alexander Souville, a Huguenot master of *trompe* architecture.

[87] Ceiling of the Hell Staircase by Antonio Verrio, with a dramatic depiction of a fire-breathing monster as the mouth of Hell, one of Verrio's most striking concepts.

[88] The Hell Staircase, as completed by the 9th Earl and 1st Marquess. The latter commissioned Thomas Stothard to paint the wall murals in a seamless match to Verrio's work above, but more Rubenesque in subject and colours.

CHAPTER III

— Georgian Glory —

THE FIRST HALF OF THE EIGHTEENTH century was a period of retrenchment at Burghley as the 6th Earl struggled to pay the debts he had inherited. He had to seek two private Acts of Parliament to dispose of entailed property. Land in north Lincolnshire amounting to over three thousand acres, and part of the Snape estate in Yorkshire, and other capital sales were undertaken, and mortgages acquired. The 6th Earl, despite his classical education, the tutoring of Matthew Prior, and his Grand Tour, did not share his parents' cultivated tastes. It was said of him that he was 'a gentleman who never was yet in business, loves hawking, horse matches [racing] and other Country sports'. The one enthusiasm of his father's which he perpetuated at Burghley was the Little Bedlam Club, the meetings of which he revived. Devoting his life to rural sports, he was content to leave his parents' achievement untouched and unfinished. Fortunately the 5th Earl had entailed his collection so it survived. The 6th Earl died in 1721 and was succeeded by his eldest son John as 7th Earl, but he only lived another four months, and was succeeded in turn by his younger brother Brownlow (named after his mother's family, of Belton House) in 1722. With him, there was a revival of low-key activity at Burghley with the acquisition of new furniture for some of the rooms, mainly from local businesses in Stamford, but also a set of three crested, gilt-framed pier glasses with candle sconces by the London maker Phineas Evans made in 1727 to 1728, for the ground floor drawing room.

The 8th Earl saved the estate by marrying an heiress, Hannah Sophia Chambers, in 1724. She was the daughter of a very rich manufacturer and merchant, trading in copper and lead. Her money went a long way to pay off the debts encumbering the property and to provide the wherewithal for a new burst of improvements at the house. Her father Thomas Chambers (1660–1726) was an opulent London merchant but hailed from Derbyshire where he owned copper foundries and also made money from Cornish mining, and was Governor of the Company of Copper Miners of England. He had, in addition, significant investments in the East India Company. He was happy to use his fortune to fund the marriage of his daughter into the aristocracy. Chambers owned the largest house in Derby which was occupied by Bonnie Prince Charles in 1745 and there the Pretender took the fatal decision not to proceed to London but to turn back and return to Scotland. This substantial town house was inherited by his daughter and renamed Exeter House but sold after the 8th Earl's death in 1758.[8]

A sign of his wealth and generosity is the enormous silver wine cistern made by Philip Rollos which he gave to Hannah and her husband as a wedding present. It bears the 8th Earl's arms impaled with Chambers for his wife, (the Chambers arms are Ermine three copper cakes with a cannon in the chief and the crest is a copper miner) referring to the source of the Chambers' wealth.

After their inheritance the Exeters visited Derby from time to time and all the church bells were rung to greet their visits. They gave a magnificent set of church plates by the London silversmith George Wickes to All Saints Derby at the time it was rebuilt to the design of James Gibbs.

Lord Exeter commissioned an inventory of the contents of Burghley in 1738, which is useful for illuminating the later stages of the 5th Earl and Countess's furnishings. It lists changes since the 1688 inventory and was probably more a record of the last fifteen years of acquisition by the 5th Earl and Countess, rather than anything of the 6th Earl's. The 8th Earl and his rich heiress wife did commission some art. The Anglo-Dutch artist Hermann van der Mijn (1684–1741) was at Burghley in 1738 and painted the two beautiful still lives *A Rose and Glass* and *A Spaniel with Game*. The 9th Earl annotated the inventory in his own hand with regard to the latter to record that the spaniel was 'Lord Exeter's favourite

dog, Diddle'. One architectural change by the 8th Earl was to move the baroque bust of Charles II by Honoré Pelle from the Marble Hall and place it in the upper archway of the East Frontispiece where it looks very well. Apart from instituting a detailed inventory of the contents and commissioning some more pictures including family portraits and the van der Mijn still lifes, and adding magnificent silver like the Rollos wine cooler from her father and customary gifts of plate as Hereditary Almoner at the coronation of George II, the 8th Earl and Countess did not make any further changes to the house and left the George Rooms unfinished in 1700.

The 5th Earl and Countess having completed Verrio's ceilings intended to hang the walls of the George Rooms with tapestries. On their last Grand Tour they again stayed in Paris and visited the Gobelins factory which by that date was concentrating solely on tapestry. There they commissioned a further set from Jan Jans (1644–1723), the Flemish manager of Gobelins with whom they maintained a working relationship for over twenty years, having commissioned the *Metamorphoses* series in 1686. Their patronage of Gobelins was part of a programme of tapestries for the new rooms that also included several from the English Mortlake and Vanderbank manufactories. Their preference was for John Vanderbank's Soho factory (an offshoot of Mortlake) in London, from which they acquired half a dozen excellent sets. All three tapestry factories produced work of similar quality as all were run by skilled Flemish weavers, though Gobelins also benefitted from lavish royal patronage which Mortlake lacked after the fall of James II; the English factory closed in 1703 following some years of struggle. It was probably for this reason that the Exeters in 1700 commissioned their last and grandest series of tapestries in Paris, a set of the *Anciennes Indes* series from a design for which only one set had hitherto been made, for Louis XIV. They were based on paintings by Albert Eckhout of the *Flora and Fauna of Brazil*, a landmark of European scientific engagement

[89] *previous pages* Burghley in its landscape setting with lake and carefully planted trees, designed by Capability Brown for Brownlow, 9th Earl of Exeter.

[90] *opposite* The large silver wine cistern by Philip Rollos, a wedding present to the 8th Earl and his heiress wife Hannah Sophia Chambers from her father, Thomas Chambers, a copper millionaire. The new Chambers arms proudly impaled with Cecil on the cistern show ingots of copper: a documented example of Georgian pride in entrepreneurial achievement. Her fortune saved the estate.

[91] *right* A detail of the 1738 Inventory commissioned by the 8th Earl which records all the 5th Earl's acquisitions integrated into the rooms at Burghley as intended.

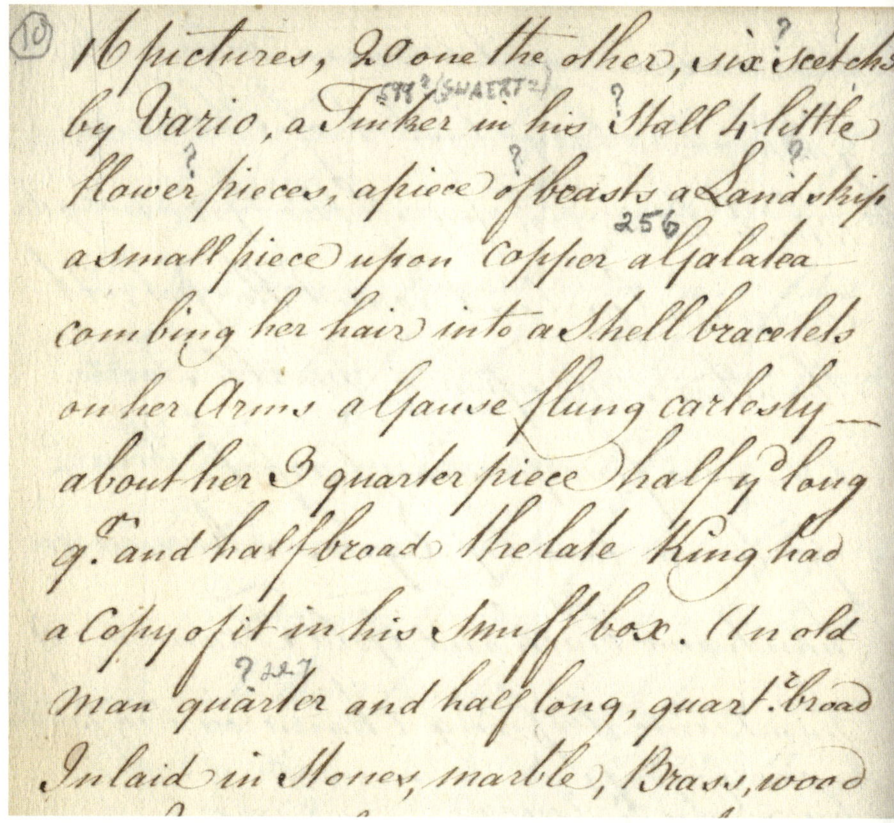
(10) 16 pictures, 20 one the other, six scetchs
by Vario, a Tinker in his Stall 4 little
flower pieces, a piece of beasts a Landship
a small piece upon Copper a Galatea
combing her hair into a Shell bracelets
on her Arms a Gause flung carlesly
about her 3 quarter piece half y long
q. and half broad the late King had
a Copy of it in his Snuff box. An old
Man quarter and half long, quart. broad
Inlaid in Money, marble, Brass, wood

with the marvels of the New World. The Eckhout cartoons were given to Louis XIV by Maurice of Nassau in 1679 for use at Gobelins. In choosing this series the Exeters were in the forefront of the grandest European patronage of the time. The *Anciennes Indes* were almost certainly intended for the State Drawing Room (Third George Room) but had hardly been started when Lord Exeter died in Paris in 1700. Lady Exeter confirmed the order, but the outbreak of the War of the Spanish Succession in 1701 prevented the delivery of the tapestries, and they never arrived at Burghley. The 6th Earl, overwhelmed by debt, made no effort to retrieve or pay for them after peace and trade were restored by the Treaty of Utrecht in 1713.

This period of stasis came to an end on the death of the 8th Earl in 1754 and the succession of his son, also called Brownlow, as 9th Earl of Exeter (1725–1793). He had married another heiress, Letitia Townshend, the daughter of the Hon. Horatio Townshend from Norfolk, though she was not as rich as his mother Hannah Sophia Chambers. Letitia died young in 1756, two years after becoming Lady Exeter, leaving her personal fortune to her son. The new Lord Exeter was a remarkable man in whom many of the good family traits were revived. He was as great an art patron and collector as the 5th Earl and Countess. He added to the library and art collection, carried out ambitious architectural improvements and had a wide love of music. He regularly organised concerts and musical events at Burghley and in London. He was also a very good businessman with extraordinary attention to detail unlike his immediate predecessors; doubtless he inherited the Chambers' entrepreneurial genes. One of his projects was the urban redevelopment of the Exeter Exchange in the Strand, London, on the site of Exeter House where Lord Burghley had died in 1598. The Elizabethan house had been demolished by the 5th Earl in the 1670s to make way for leasing the site to Nicholas Barbon, the rather sharp building entrepreneur responsible for Seven Dials and parts of southern Bloomsbury. As 'fashion' moved westward, with the development of St. James's by the Crown after the Restoration and then Mayfair by the Berkeley and Grosvenor Estates, the former Tudor and Stuart great houses (on the site of medieval bishops' palaces) along the Strand facing the river were redeveloped in the 1670s by their owners as streets of houses and commercial premises, including Arundel House by the 6th Duke of Norfolk, Durham Place, and York House by the 2nd Duke of Buckingham. Only Northumberland House held out until its demolition to make way for Northumberland Avenue in the 1870s. Barbon with the 5th Earl's trustees Francis Child, the banker, and the Duke of Devonshire, built Exeter Exchange as one of the first purely commercial blocks in the West End with small shops, mainly occupied by milliners, on the ground floor and a warehouse above used by the Company of Upholsterers and John Gumley, the leading manufacturer of looking glasses who made two enormous pier glasses for the Duke of Devonshire's state rooms at Chatsworth.

As redeveloped by the 9th Earl, the ground floor became one of the first shopping arcades with a central gallery flanked by small outlets, a forerunner of the Burlington Arcade, and the upper floor a concert room. There Giovanni Battista Gervasio (1725–1785), the Neapolitan composer and virtuoso mandolinist, gave his first London concert in 1768, but from 1773 it was adapted as the popular visitor attraction Clark's Menagerie with a lion and lioness, monkeys, parrots

[92] Hermann van der Mijn, *Still Life with Spaniel and Game*, commissioned by the 8th Earl, one of two works by the artist at Burghley. The 9th Earl recorded that the spaniel Diddle was his father's favourite dog.

and a famous elephant called Chunee, who having been friendly, embracing visitors with his trunk, went mad and violent in his old age and had to be shot by soldiers in 1826 whereupon the remaining animals were transferred to the new London Zoo in Regents Park. This urban redevelopment at Exeter Exchange was one of the ways in which the 9th Earl nurtured the family fortune, and as a result was in a position to continue and complete the great scheme for the interior and setting of Burghley. His business-like approach and close control of detail were reflected in the commissioning of a new inventory of contents in 1763 which he and his staff kept up-to-date until his death thirty years later.

The 9th Earl was educated at Winchester and St. John's College, Cambridge. He sat as MP for Rutland from 1747 until he succeeded his father in 1754 and moved to the House of Lords, and was Lord Lieutenant of Rutland from 1751 to 1779. He was described by Horace Walpole as 'a man of good understanding', which was high praise from that quarter. He followed in the footsteps of the 5th Earl and went on two Grand Tours to collect art when in his forties. Whereas the 5th Earl and Countess worked together, acting as a team to achieve the baroque transformation of Burghley, the 9th Earl was solely responsible for his programme in the park and house which began following the death of his wife in 1756. That was the year he engaged Capability Brown to start work at Burghley as both his landscape designer and architect. It seems likely that Lord Exeter embarked that year on the improvements as a consolation and occupation in his bereavement. Though he didn't share his project with a spouse, he was close to his sister Lady Betty Chaplin, who helped him running the house and estate for fifteen years and shared his unusual degree of competence. During his absences in Italy he left Lady Betty in charge of Burghley with full powers of direction, and gave her detailed authority over his agent, Mr. Hurst, and instructions in his own hand before he left for the Continent on 10 July 1768. Lady Betty was to act for him on a wide range of matters: church-livings, charities and donations, estate management including game and the kitchen garden, general building-maintenance, but above all the completion of his building and furnishing while he was away. These instructions reveal much about Lord Exeter, particularly his seriousness, priorities, foresight, decency and intelligent grasp of practical matters. He even suggested names for staff replacements in case of the death of existing incumbents.

Lady Betty was to visit Burghley every summer without notice to check that 'everything is kept neat both in the house and garden'. The farm, horses and fowls were all to be taken care of, and she was to ensure 'as few trees as possible be cut down in Burghley Park'. There are fascinating details about housekeeping and looking after the collection. 'Mr. Hurst will take care that my orders for lighting fires often in all the north rooms at Burghley are follow'd, once a week

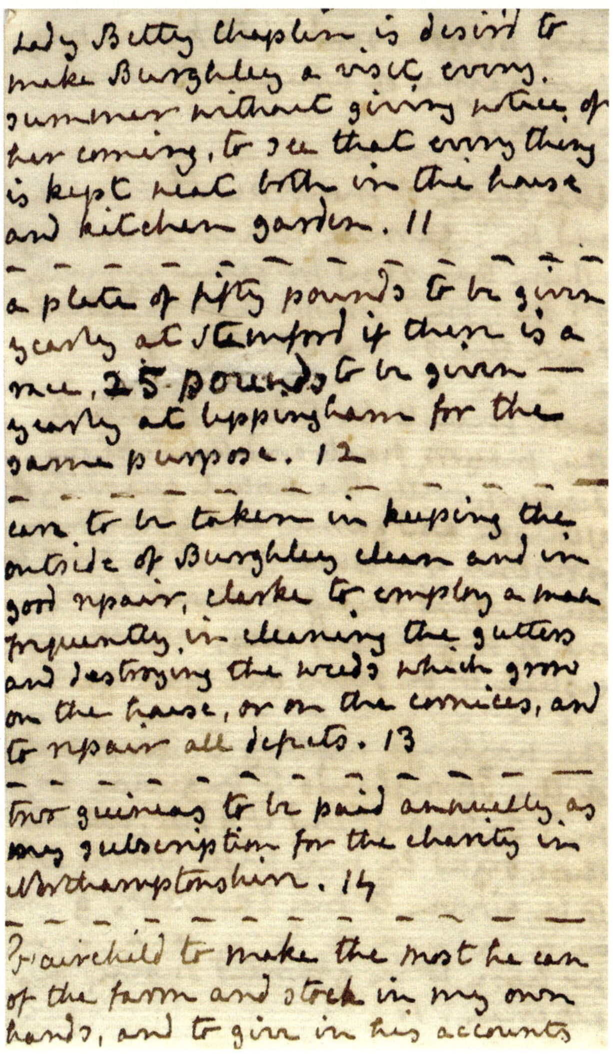

Lady Betty Chaplin is desir'd to make Burghley a visit every summer without giving notice of her coming, to see that every thing is kept neat both in the house and kitchen garden. 11

a plate of fifty pounds to be given yearly at Stamford if there is a race, 25 pounds to be given — yearly at Uppingham for the same purpose. 12

care to be taken in keeping the outside of Burghley clean and in good repair, clarke to employ a man frequently in cleaning the gutters and destroying the weeds which grow on the house, or on the cornices, and to repair all defects. 13

two guineas to be paid annually as my subscription for the charity in Northamptonshire. 14

Fairchild to make the most he can of the farm and stock in my own hands, and to give in his accounts

[93] *left* Pastel portrait by John Russell RA of Lady Betty Chaplin, the sister of the 9th Earl, who helped him at Burghley after the death of his wife.

[94] *below left* Notes from the 9th Earl to his sister Lady Betty, with instructions for completing his improvements and general management of the house and estate at Burghley while he was away on his Grand Tour.

at least during damp weather in each room, and to have one frequently in the room where the valuables are left'.

Lord Exeter trusted his sister to understand his intentions for the works in hand. The dining room was to be wainscoted and painted. Lady Betty was to 'paper Nan's Room' with the yellow paper from Bromwich (the leading London wallpaper manufacturer) and to choose the wallpaper herself for the Chapel Bedroom in the north-east corner of the house where work was underway in the 1760s, including the creation of the chapel where the furniture was being made to an appropriate gothick design by the leading London firm of Mayhew and Ince. Lady Betty was exhorted to 'hasten Mr. Mayhew for Chapel furniture' and ensure that the room leading to the Chapel was hung in crimson fabric. The other area being worked on was the ground floor on the north front with the new library (replacing that in the demolished north wing), and a spacious new entrance hall. The two gilt framed pier glasses ordered from Mayhew and Ince were to be hung in the library when delivered and 'if the pillers in my North Hall have done sweating before my return Lady Betty will order Bertoli [Domenico Bartoli, the scagliola specialist] down to repair and new polish them'.

The architect for these new works was Capability Brown (1716–1783) who was employed by Lord Exeter from 1756 to 1779 at a cost of £10,000. Brown's foreman on site from 1764 to 1779 was William Ireland. Brown told Lord Harcourt of Nuneham Courtenay that he 'had twenty-five years pleasure restoring the monument of a great minister of a great Queen'. He was employed in the first instance to landscape the park, but Lord Exeter soon realised that, with his eye for picturesque aesthetics and admiration for the scenic and theatrical possibilities of architecture, Brown was most suitable to work on the house with sensitivity and due appreciation for Lord Burghley's masterpiece.

Brown came to public attention as head gardener to Lord Cobham at Stowe where he acted as clerk of works as well as

Brownlow Earl Exeter

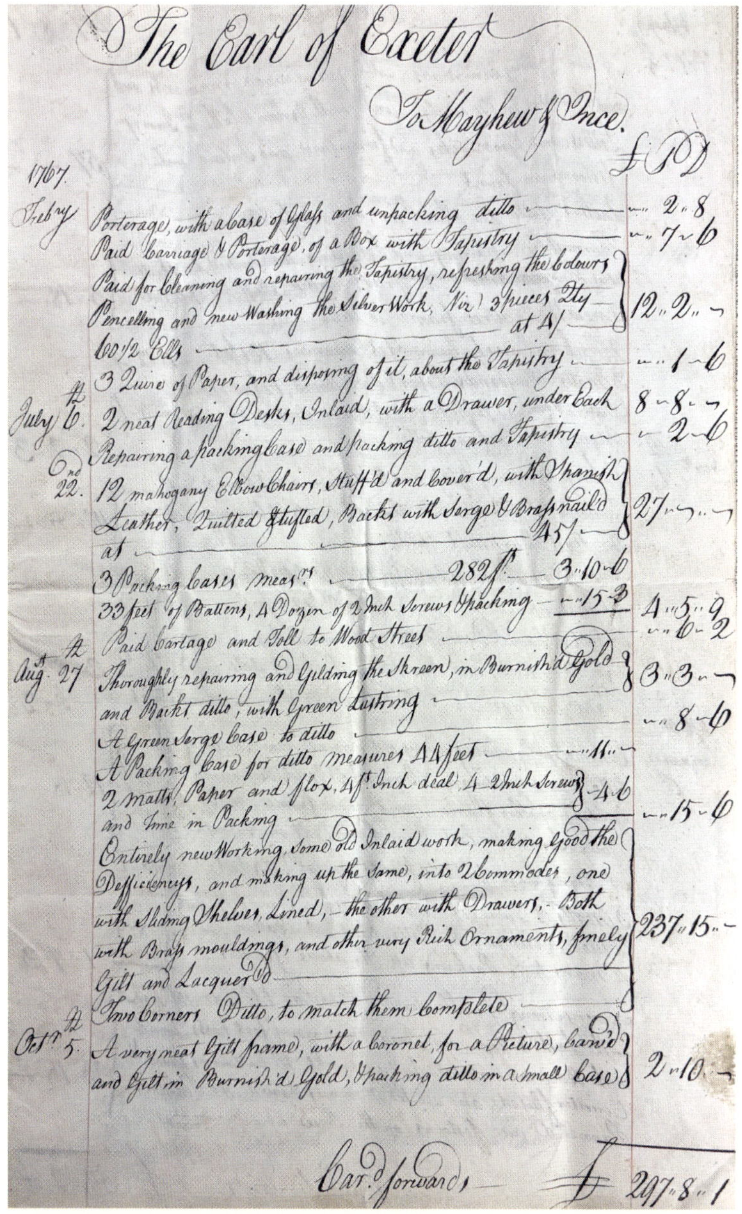
The Earl of Exeter
To Mayhew & Ince.

1767		£ s d
Feby	Porterage, with a Case of Glass and unpacking ditto	2.8
	Paid Carriage & Porterage, of a Box with Tapestry	7.6
	Paid for Cleaning and repairing the Tapestry, refreshing the Colours, Pencelling and new Washing the Silver Work, Viz 3 pieces Qty 60½ Ells at 4/	12.2.–
	3 Quire of Paper, and disposing of it, about the Tapestry	1.6
July 6	2 neat Reading Desks, Inlaid, with a Drawer, under Each	8.8.–
	Repairing a Packing Case and packing ditto and Tapestry	2.6
22	12 mahogany Elbow Chairs, Stuff'd and Cover'd, with Spanish Leather, Quilted & Stuffed, Backs with Serge & Brass nail'd at 45/	27.–.–
	3 Packing Cases meas.d 282 ft 3.10.6; 33 feet of Battens, 4 Dozen of 2 Inch Screws & Packing 15.3	4.5.9
	Paid Cartage and Toll to Wood Street	6.2
Aug 27	Thoroughly repairing and Gilding the Skreen, in Burnish'd Gold and Back't ditto, with Green Lustring	3.3.–
	A Green Serge Case to ditto	8.6
	A Packing Case for ditto measures 44 feet 11.–; 2 matts, Paper and flox, 4 ft Inch deal, 4 2 Inch Screws and Time in Packing 4.6	15.6
	Entirely new Working, some old Inlaid work, making good the Defficiencys, and making up the same, into 2 Commodes, one with Sliding Shelves, Lined, the other with Drawers, Both with Brass mouldings, and other very Rich Ornaments, finely Gilt and Lacquer'd. Two Corners Ditto, to match them Compleate	237.15.–
Octr 5	A very neat Gilt frame, with a Coronet, for a Picture, carved and Gilt in Burnish'd Gold, & packing ditto in a small Case	2.10.–
	Carr.d forward £	297.8.1

[95] *opposite* Angelica Kauffman, *Portrait of Brownlow, the 9th Earl of Exeter*. Painted in 1763 at Naples while on his Grand Tour, where he settled for some time and was introduced to the artistic milieu in the city by Angelica and the British Minister in Naples, Sir William Hamilton.

[96] *right* Bill from Mayhew and Ince for the new furniture for Burghley commissioned by the 9th Earl in the 1760s and 1770s. They worked in a variety of styles, from Baroque to Neo-classical, following Lord Exeter's direction.

[97] *below right* Commode by Mayhew and Ince with ormolu mounts and rosewood, yew and purple heart marquetry, commissioned by the 9th Earl for the George Rooms.

gardening. At Stowe he cooperated with William Kent, the architect and the first great exponent of English landscape gardening, in naturalizing the existing formal garden. As Lord Cobham's gardener, Brown was asked by others to advise on their grounds, and after Lord Cobham's death he gave up his post at Stowe and set up as a landscape consultant and architect, soon establishing a pre-eminent reputation in his field. Capability Brown worked in collaboration with the London master-builder Henry Holland (who became Brown's son-in-law, and was father of the fashionable Whig architect Henry Holland) so was able to do contracting as well as designing. His career was a heartening success story, he made a fortune, bought an estate at Fenstanton in Huntingdonshire and sent his son to Eton where he was nicknamed 'Capie', such was the fame of his father. Unlike Talman or Verrio, Capability Brown was easy to get on with and became and remained friends with his clients. Lord Exeter chose his designer sensibly.

Capability Brown designed new stables, a greenhouse and a banqueting house, in a William Kent–inspired gothick vein, although the latter garden building paid deference to the Elizabethan scenario and derived its details from the Banqueting House at Chipping Campden in Gloucestershire which belonged to Lord Exeter's Rutland neighbour the Earl of Gainsborough of Exton (the successor to the Royalist Viscount Campden). It was erected in 1787 by John and Robert Hames, masons. All these buildings were offshoots of Brown's plan for the park to form an ideal setting for Lord Burghley's masterpiece, sweeping away the remnants of the 5th Earl's formal London and Wise layout, which had already been simplified to reduce costs of maintenance during the 6th Earl's financial retrenchment. It is due to the 9th Earl and Brown that the house, in Pevsner's words, sits in 'supreme self-confidence on the wide lawns of its eighteenth century garden'.

[98] Nathaniel Dance, *Portrait of Capability Brown*. Lord Exeter first employed Brown in 1756 and they worked together for twenty-five years to perfect the architecture of the house, create the designed landscape in which it sits, and design subsidiary buildings including the stables, orangery, bridge and garden structures.

Brown was a genius and an artist, as was understood by Humphry Repton, who explained how Brown became one of the most original creative minds of the eighteenth century. Though Brown had no early professional training, as a result of his 'access to the principal houses of the country, his intercourse with men of genius and science, his natural quickness of perception and his habitual correctness of observation, he became acquainted with the "higher requisites of art, relating to form, to proportion, to character, and above all to arrangement"'. These were the qualities Brown displayed to perfection in the transformation of the setting of the Elizabethan house. He immediately grasped the spectacular theatrical impact of the architecture and set about the surroundings to make it appear more prominent with the illusion that it was on an eminence rather than low down in relatively flat country. The ground was contoured, to establish wide lawns in the foreground contrived to show the full extent of the building, and to variegate the middle ground with slopes and clumped planting. The north wing (containing the old library) was demolished to expose the full scale of the north and west fronts as a continuous picturesque composition with the obelisk clock tower serving as a *Stadtkrone* rising above the long, variegated elevations. A lake covering twenty-two acres was dug, curving around to the south, at just the right distance from the house, and enclosing the pleasure grounds to the east. The earth excavated from the lake was used to build new hills to the south-east which were planted with shrubs, flowering plants, and cedars amidst winding paths. The Campden banqueting house formed a *point de vue* there, overlooking the eastern part of the lake. To the north-east a new Gothic stable block was constructed round an open court, impressively expanding the outbuildings in that direction. Some way south of the stable block was an orangery facing the pleasure grounds, also gothic in design. Nearer the house clumps of oak, beech and limes were planted, and further away large sweeping belts of mixed trees drew the eye outwards. The extensive brick-walled kitchen gardens a mile away towards the south-east boundary were enlarged and concealed there by more planting. Everything was on a massive scale. All ancient trees were retained and incorporated into the augmented planting schemes.

The London and Wise avenues to north and south—Queen Anne's Avenue—were preserved, no doubt at Lord Exeter's wish. Brown's aesthetic judgment was guided by Lord Exeter's own love of old trees. The seemingly casual planting was dictated by Brown's scientific knowledge of the ground and soil as well as dendrology, with different species being planted on clay, or gravel, or alluvial soil, depending on where they would flourish best. Views and buildings were enclosed by clumps or individual specimen trees, and long and short vistas contrived which hid and revealed the house in a kinetic sequence from the approach drives. Longer vistas were focused on local landmarks including the spire of Stamford St. Martin one and a quarter miles to the north-west. From the south and west fronts carefully framed vistas drew the eye along the lake. These views were gloriously enhanced by the construction of the Lion Bridge built to Brown's design in 1775 which, as well as being a major object, gave views to or from the house through its segmental arches, making one of the most memorable landscape set pieces in the park. It was perfectly sited and aligned on a skew to make it prominent from the house. Horace Walpole wrote after a visit in 1763: 'A noble Pile! Brown is ornamenting the Park and has built a gothic greenhouse and stables which are not bad but they do not accord with the house which is not Gothic.' Walpole slightly misunderstood, as while the main quadrangle is Elizabethan Renaissance, Lord Burghley's Great Hall to the east is Gothic with pointed and traceried windows and steep pitched roof, and Brown was relating to that in his adjoining work. The Orangery, for instance, repeated in *diminuendo* the glazing and the turrets of the Hall. On the whole, Brown's work has always been admired. The 1815 Guide Book wrote 'the changes unquestionably add greatly to the grandeur of the house'.

Brown also made extensive adjustments to the exterior of Burghley, but his touches are so sensitive and 'in-keeping' that the eye barely notices them. All the Elizabethan mullioned and transomed windows in the external elevations were sashed, with a slight gothick touch in the glazing bars. This continued the reglazing begun by the 5th Earl. All new or extended windows copied the Elizabethan originals. On the south front, Brown raised the whole centre in 1760, creating a dummy second storey with larger mullioned and transomed windows to match the lower storey, disguising the extra height of the George Rooms within and lining up with Lord Burghley's flanking sections. Different patterns of balustrade were considered including crenellation, but as executed a continuous balustrade was adopted, its pattern taken from that in the inner courtyard. This created the even symmetry beloved of Georgian taste. In the process the original frilled top dressing of the centre bays with little arches and miniature obelisks reflecting that of the flanking 'towers' disappeared, which is slightly regrettable. Interestingly, the south front—so majestic, so evenly composed, and so Elizabethan-looking—is as much a creation of the eighteenth century as of the sixteenth. The work to the outside was a natural part of Brown's work, concomitant with the landscaping of the grounds, to increase the scenic impact and can be judged in that capacity, with the removal of a wing here, or the addition of a skyline there, like touches to an oil painting.

Capability Brown was also employed to remodel the interior of the house. His work affected the ground floor rooms on the north front and the chapel and bedrooms on the first floor adjoining the Roman Stairs and Great Kitchen in the north-east corner of the quadrangle. The chapel was given a thin-ribbed 'Elizabethan' stucco ceiling designed by Brown. As has been seen from the written instructions given to Lady Betty when Lord Exeter left on his second Grand Tour in 1768, these changes were underway then, and succeeded the external landscaping and architectural titivation as the annual programme rolled forward. The two phases—the park after 1756 and the interior after 1764—followed Lord Exeter's inheritances from his wife and mother.

Lord Dacre of Belhus in Essex, one of Brown's earliest clients, had written to his friend Sanderson Miller, the gentleman architect and antiquary, at the beginning of the Burghley campaign that Capability Brown 'tells me that he has the alterations of Burleigh and that not only of the Park but of the house which wherever it is Gothick he intends to preserve in that State and whatever ornaments he adds are to be so'. Lord Dacre added that Brown wanted to consult Sanderson Miller for his opinion. This demonstrates that the architectural changes to the house were planned from the start and formed part of the project even though executed in sequence after the landscaping. It also shows the aesthetic philosophy, tinged with antiquarianism that informed the design.

[99] *opposite above* Design by Capability Brown for remodelling the roofline of the south front, where he raised the height of the upper tier of windows and parapet to bring it into line with the flanking towers and enhance the monumental impact.

[100] *opposite below* Anthony Devis, *Watercolour of Capability Brown's Landscape*, with lake, heroic bridge, and artful clumps of trees revealing vistas to the house and emphasising its scale.

The ground floor of the north range as remodelled in 1767 to 1768 by Lord Exeter comprised a central entrance hall with a dining room to the east and the new library to the west. He continued to occupy the contiguous 5th Earl's bedroom in the west range. He admired the 'Antique' quality of the latter, cleaning the silver thread Vanderbank tapestries and reviving the 'Imperial bedstead' there—with new blue silk hangings, to harmonise with the blue and silver of the tapestries. The library and dining room were remodelled to Brown's design with up-to-date plaster ceilings based on the recent publication by Robert Wood and James Dawkins: *The Ruins of Palmyra* (1753) which Lord Exeter owned. For the hall a design was obtained in 1765 from the doyen of English neo-classicists Robert Adam who designed a characteristic 'filigree' ceiling and lined the room with Ionic 'Siena Marble' scagliola columns made by Domenico Bartoli. Scagliola is a composition of marble chips in plaster to look like true marble. It is applied to a wooden frame and takes time to dry. When dry, it is polished with pumice stones to give the shiny finish of real marble. Hence the instructions given to Lady Betty to get Bartoli back from London when the columns had finished 'sweating'. The Adam ceiling was carried out by local plasterers. This is Adam's only executed work at Burghley, though he produced a scheme for the Great Stairs. It is possible that Adam was recommended to Lord Exeter by Brown, as they had both worked together on the interiors at Croome for Lord Coventry, just before Brown moved on to Burghley. Apart from the library and Dead Bedlam on the ground floor, Brown also supplied a new 'Palmyra'-inspired ceiling design for the old 'Plaister Dining Room', now Billiard Room upstairs. Horace Walpole wrote in 1763: 'He is going through the house by degrees, finishing a room every year, and has already made several most sumptuous'.

A major component of the 9th Earl's interior work was the acquisition of new furniture from the London partnership of Mayhew and Ince which was employed at Burghley from 1767 (the date of their first bill) to 1779. In the furnishing, as in his architectural changes, the 9th Earl showed an 'unusually enlightened combination of sensitive antiquarianism on the one hand and well-informed awareness of the rising tide of neo-classicism on the other'.[9] This balance of interests was reflected in the fact that he was a Fellow of the Society of Antiquaries and a Fellow of the Royal Society of Arts. The latter's headquarters in the Adelphi was designed by Adam, which was another channel through which the architect might have been introduced to Lord Exeter. Mayhew and Ince were also working at Croome so may have come from there through the Brown-Adam recommendation. Mayhew and Ince's contribution, dictated by Lord Exeter's taste, was remarkably various. They reconstructed the beds in a baroque spirit. The pier glasses in the library were austerely neo-classical with Grecian wreaths on top (they are still there between the windows), whereas Mayhew and Ince's *gilt* frame for the overmantel glass in the Red Drawing Room on the south front was amazingly baroque, and was described in their bill as a 'rich frame'. It is certainly that.

In addition to refurnishing the family rooms, Mayhew and Ince provided lamps, lanterns and pedestals for halls and passages, and the gothic fittings and seat-furniture for the chapel, including the reading desk and pulpit there. The main dining room on the south front was enlarged to incorporate the Tea Room, utilised as a sideboard area behind a screen of Corinthian columns, and refurnished with neo-classical mahogany side tables, and matching sideboard urns, in the fashion later made popular by Adam.

Lord Exeter finally moved on to complete the George Rooms on the first floor, his major achievement at Burghley. In preparation, like the 5th Earl, he embarked on two Grand Tours of Italy. Lord Exeter travelled on his first tour in 1763 with William Patoun, who later wrote *Advice on Travel in Italy* (1766) which described some of their experiences and included

[101] *above left* Orazio Gentileschi, *Madonna and Child*. Given to the 9th Earl by Pope Clement XIV, a notable mark of respect to a Protestant Englishman.

[102] *below left* Artemisia Gentileschi, *Susanna and the Elders*, bought in Rome by the 9th Earl from the Palazzo Barberini where Princess Barberini was selling the pictures to fund her gambling habit.

[103] *opposite left & right* Cesare Aguatti, *Mosaics of the Temple of Vesta at Tivoli and the Colosseum*, purchased by the 9th Earl on his Second Grand Tour in Rome in 1774–5, through the English dealer-cicerone Thomas Jenkins.

useful details like how to choose '*cicerones*' to act as guides. Lord Exeter used James Byres (1733–1817) both as a *cicerone* and an art agent. He also used Thomas Jenkins (1722–1798), the restorer and dealer in classical antiquities, especially from the recent excavation at Hadrian's Villa, Tivoli, both on behalf of the Vatican museum and English 'Milordi'. The 9th Earl, like the 5th Earl, did not collect many Roman antiquities,[10] but concentrated on contemporary objects and sculpture including the work of Joseph Nollekens (1737–1823), who was in Rome from 1760 to 1770, and sixteenth-century Italian paintings, as well as adding to the Italian baroque art. His detailed interest is attested by the copy of Pellegrino Antonio Orlandi's *Abecedario Pittorico* (1704) in the library, which he annotated with many pictures he admired in the collections he saw. While Jenkins is sometimes dismissed as a bit of a rogue, or at the least optimistic in his attributions, Byres was well-informed and reasonably honest. Many of the works of art he sold to Grand Tourists are now in the major museums and galleries of the world like the Portland Vase in the British Museum. He had access to the Barbarini Collection where the Princess Barbarini, an incorrigible gambler, funded her vice by selling works of art from the family palazzo. Byres was able to acquire several Barbarini items for the 9th Earl which are now at Burghley. Lord Exeter commissioned the artist Nikolaus Mosmann, a pupil of Mengs to make drawings of paintings in the palace and elsewhere. Mosmann worked for Lord Exeter for thirty years drawing art in Rome, and after the artist's death in 1787 he paid Mosmann's widow a pension. Lord Exeter's patronage had a public-spirited side as well as acquiring things for Burghley. He gave the Mosmann drawings to the British Museum for general education, and also gave the fledgling museum a table incorporating a top made of Vesuvian lava. He opened the house to the general public from 1770, initiating a tradition which has lasted to the present.

In his first Grand Tour he visited Turin, Parma, Florence, Naples and Rome. In Naples he met and befriended Angelica Kauffman, to whom he was introduced by Sir William Hamilton, and who painted his portrait, by far the most sympathetic of the portraits he commissioned of himself in the course of his life. He bequeathed it to Lady Betty, and it passed to her descendants only being acquired for the Burghley Collection in recent years. He bought other work from Kauffman including several of her 'history' pieces and a portrait of the actor David Garrick, a frequent dining companion in Naples. He also bought Nathaniel Dance's portrait of Kauffman which hangs at Burghley, as does the same artist's portrait of Capability Brown as a record of two of Lord Exeter's most favoured artists. In Rome he commissioned *Lady Hamilton as Hebe feeding Jupiter's Eagle* from the British neo-classical artist Gavin Hamilton which is still at Burghley, and bought Nicolas Poussin's *Assumption of the Virgin* which was sold for death duties in 1955 and is now in the National Gallery of Art in Washington.

Four years later in 1768, having entrusted his affairs to Lady Betty he returned to Italy and revisited Naples, Rome and Venice. In Naples he commissioned four views by Pietro Fabris (finished between 1767 and 1770), and objects like lava tabletops. In Rome via James Byres and Thomas Jenkins he bought good paintings by Domenichino, Guido Reni, Sassoferato and Castiglione which complemented the 5th Earl's acquisitions at Burghley, but his seemingly more starry items—a Virgin and Child by 'Correggio' and another by 'Raphael' have turned out to be copies. Through Jenkins he commissioned *veduti* of Rome from Philipp Hackert, the German artist and friend of Goethe, in 1769 and also acquired mosaic pictures of the Colosseum and Temple of Vesta at Tivoli by Cesare Aguatti. His outstanding purchases were in Venice, including three large Paolo Veroneses from the derelict church of San Jacopo Murano. He also bought the *Adoration of the Magi* by Jacopo Bassano, now considered the outstanding painting at Burghley. The Veronese of *Zebedee's Wife Petitioning Our Lord* became the altarpiece in Lord Exeter's remodelled chapel. After his return he received in 1774 one of the most beautiful acquisitions, a *Virgin and Child* by Orazio Gentileschi, as a mark of approbation from Pope Clement XIV to whom Lord Exeter had given a telescope. He continued to correspond with Jenkins and Byers in Rome in the 1770s, and several works continued to arrive at Burghley after he was back in England. As well as paintings, sculpture by Nollekens, marbles and modern mosaics, he acquired sixteenth-century majolica, an unusual and discerning taste for a late-Georgian English collector.

Having acquired these further Grand Tour augmentations to the already exceptionally large collection at Burghley, the 9th Earl finally embarked on the completion of the 5th Earl's George Rooms which had been left unfinished apart from the Dressing Room with its Grinling Gibbons carvings. The intention was to render them, as the 5th Earl and Countess had intended, as a Pitti Palace sequence of state rooms arranged as art galleries. Verrio's ceilings were there but no floors and no wall coverings. Work was now continuous up to the Earl's death. Floors were laid, not of

[104] *left* Paolo Veronese, *Zebedee's Wife Petitioning Christ with God the Father in Glory*. Altarpiece from the church of San Jacopo, Murano, Venice. Bought by the 9th Earl, together with two panels of St. James and St. Augustine, in June 1769. It was intended to be and still is the altarpiece in the chapel at Burghley.

[105] *opposite* Robert Adam, *Unexecuted Design for the Hell Staircase*. This scheme for completing the decoration of the walls was commissioned by the 9th Earl, who in the event used a local man, Thomas Lumby, for the cantilevered imperial plan stairs erected in 1786.

parquet de Versailles but with planks of Baltic pine. The walls of the State Bedroom were hung with three of the 5th Earl and Countess's tapestries which were in store in the 1688 Inventory. They are Soho Tapestries of the Elements—Fire, Water, Air—by John Vanderbank after designs by Lebrun, with the unique details of portraits of Burghley House and Wothorpe in rectangular panels in the borders, as well as the arms of the 5th Earl and Countess at the top.

The Drawing Room was lined with red damask, as a background to spectacular Italian paintings. The Dining Room was lined with oak wainscot like the Dressing Room. The joinery was completed to match the seventeenth-century work in the Dressing Room and Gallery Rooms. The only noticeable difference is that the Georgian doorcases are finished with cornices and not with full entablatures richly carved by Grinling Gibbons or Maine and Young, like the seventeenth-century work. The cornices repeat the gilded acanthus carving of the Dressing Room, and it is not entirely clear whether they are the 5th Earl's or the 9th Earl's, as they form an essential base for the coves of the painted ceilings. The chimneypieces, however, are all the 9th Earl's including that in the Dressing Room which is a neat neo-classical design inlaid with delicate inlays of antique granite and coloured marble by John Augustus Richter (1730–1809). The chef d'oeuvre is that in the State Bedroom, the Second George Room which is a magnificent affair by Giovanni Battista Piranesi (1720–1778) acquired in Rome via Jenkins. It is embellished with Rosso Antico marble reliefs which Jenkins claimed were antiquities excavated from Hadrian's Villa at Tivoli but might just as well be by a contemporary Roman sculptor, and none the worse for that. The chimneypiece in the Third George Room, the State Drawing Room, is also a neo-classical show-stopper, of white marble inlaid with coloured scagliola by Richter, who was in partnership with Bartoli. In 1770 he took out a patent for a 'Method of inlaying Scagliola in and upon marble'. This chimneypiece may have been designed by Robert Adam as Richter often worked for him though he could design himself. It is close to Adam's work; at the time he produced the designs for the North Hall and Great Stairs. Over it is a Medusa Head by Nollekens commissioned in Rome and placed in this position by the 9th Earl where the wall is hollowed behind to enable it to site on the mantel shelf.

The 9th Earl's completion of the George Rooms is remarkable for its sensitivity to the original design. He was not unique in this, and his work parallels George III's refurbishment of the State Apartments at Windsor Castle with the retention

and augmentation of Verrio's ceilings and Grinling Gibbons carvings there. Even so, the 9th Earl's work was remarkable for its date in being so sympathetic to the baroque, and in his deliberate antiquarianism based, he said, on study of books of old architecture and ornament in his library, as well as repeating details of the existing treatment in the seventeenth-century interiors. Capability Brown was not involved in this stage at Burghley, and Lord Exeter himself decorated and supervised the finishing of the George Rooms, incorporating chimneypieces that he had commissioned in Rome and London, and hanging there the largest and grandest of the 5th Earl's paintings, amplified by those he had collected himself. He employed a London firm to execute the joinery, including wainscot and door frames, and provide furniture: Fell and Newton, cabinet makers of Wardour Street. Their names first appear in the Burghley Day Books in 1781. They worked there until 1804, finishing the work for the 10th Earl (later 1st Marquess). Their bills came to over £10,000. The apogee of their work was the carved and gilded state bed with an elaborate baldachino on rich supports with free-standing corner pedestals. (The bed survives with modifications.) It is possible that the carving and gilding was executed by Edward Wyatt who was employed by Fell and Newton as a sub-contractor at that time, and did work in the royal palaces for George III and Prince Regent.

The 9th Earl's antiquarian sensitivity, combining baroque with up-to-date neo-classicism, is also manifested in some of the furniture made for him by Mayhew and Ince. In the Third George Room is a set of commodes and corner cupboards composed of panels of floral marquetry reused

[106] *below* Jacopo Bassano, *The Adoration of the Magi*. Painted in 1537, bought by the 9th Earl in Venice. It is one of the most important pictures in the collection.

[107] *opposite* Capability Brown's lake and lion bridge, erected in 1778.

from the floor of the 5th Countess's Dressing Room on the ground floor, mounted in fashionable neo-classical ormolu, a characteristic commission of the 9th Earl's. The centre-piece of the Dressing Room floor was made into a tabletop. Thomas Blore in his guidebook to Burghley confirms that the rooms were finished using details supplied by the 9th Earl and that the wainscot was executed by Newton under his 'express direction'.

The work on the south side was completed by the Great Stairs erected to an imperial plan as always intended. This is based on Adam's suggested arrangement with a centred bottom flight leading to a half landing at the level of the Great Hall with two symmetrical return flights to an upper landing (supported on Roman Doric columns) giving access to the Heaven Room and the enfilade of four succeeding George Rooms making a suitable grand approach. The Stairs were executed by the local architect Thomas Lumby (1755–1804) in 1786. He also worked for the Burghley estate on the design of new houses at Stamford. He was a good mason, responsible for the wafer-thin elegance of the cantilevered stone treads. The simple bronze trellis-design balustrade was made by the London metal worker William Johnson. Adam's scheme for the upper wall decoration was never executed though the rusticated treatment of the ground floor dates from 1786, and it was left for the 1st Marquess, who inherited in 1793 to employ Thomas Stothard (1755–1834) to complete the walls with appropriate paintings complementing Verrio's dramatic 'Hell' ceiling.

[108] *previous pages*
The Pleasure Grounds, with cedar trees and a banqueting house inspired by that at Chipping Campden in Gloucestershire.

[109] *right*
The South Front, with Capability Brown's upper windows and continuous balustrade, a characteristic piece of Georgian architectural tidying.

[110] The North Entrance Hall as remodelled by the 9th Earl, with a stucco ceiling designed by Robert Adam and scagliola columns by Domenico Bartoli, the polishing of which Lord Exeter entrusted to Lady Betty to supervise.

[111] The 9th Earl's Library, with stucco ceiling designed by Capability Brown. The 5th and 9th Earls formed an important collection of books on art and architecture.

[112] From the Roman Stairs to the Billiard Room on the first floor of the north range.

[113] The Billiard Room, designed by Capability Brown, with the ceiling inspired by recent discoveries at Palmyra.

[114] John Powell (after Thomas Hudson), *Portrait of Letitia Townshend, wife of the 9th Earl*, who died young in 1756 after only eight years of marriage.

[115] The Billiard Room, with oval framed portraits of members of the 5th Earl's Little Bedlam Club.

[116] The superb chimneypiece by Giovanni Battista Piranesi in the Second George Room, commissioned by the 9th Earl in Rome.

[117] Detail of Piranesi's chimneypiece in the Second George Room. The rosso-antico tablets supplied by Bartolomeo Cavaceppi, the dealer-restorer, were said to come from Hadrian's Villa at Tivoli.

[118] Verrio's ceiling in the Second George Room above the state bed supplied by Fell and Newton in 1790, its cornice carved (possibly by Edward Wyatt) with doves in a wreath symbolising marital love.

[119] Detail of Verrio's ceiling, depicting Mercury.

HONOR
PVLCHERRIMA
MERCES IPSE SIBI

[120] The Third George Room as completed by the 9th Earl in the 1770s. Only Verrio's ceiling depicting the Reconciliation of Cupid and Psyche had been executed; the walls were hung by the 9th Earl with red damask (renewed recently) as a background to the 5th Earl's Italian paintings with augmentations of his own. The 9th Earl also commissioned the inlaid marble Bartoli and Richter chimneypiece, which may have been designed by Robert Adam.

[121] The Third George Room reflected in a looking glass.

[122] *left & right*
A recreation of the 9th Earl's picture hang masterminded by John Somerville and Alec Cobbe; which was a completion of the 5th Earl's intentions inspired by the Pitti Palace in Florence and the Barberini Palace in Rome.

512
67
11
231
461

[123] *left & right* Details of Verrio's ceiling painting in the Third George Room, showing his mastery of human form and beautiful colours. The subject is Cupid and Psyche.

[124] *left & right*
Details of the inlaid marble work by Bartoli and Richter in the chimneypiece of the Third George Room. The marble bust of Medea is by Joseph Nollekens and was bought from him in Rome by the 9th Earl in 1764.

[125] The Fourth George Room, the state dining room, with convincing oak panelling inserted by the 9th Earl in the 1770s, and made by the London firm of Fell and Newton.

[126] A corner of the Fourth George Room looking beyond the painting of Judith with the Head of Holofernes by Elisabetta Sirani.

[127] Urbania Majolica Vase, dated 1670, and antique Roman marble and Vesuvius lava tabletop; both acquired in the 1760s by the 9th Earl on his Grand Tour. He gave a similar tabletop to the British Museum for general education.

[128] *left & right*
Details of Verrio's ceiling in the Fourth George Room, which depicts a Feast of the Gods. The seafood and coral still life is especially attractive.

[129] Studio of Giovanni Francesco Barbieri, called Guercino, *The Triumph of David*, over a side table in the Fourth George Room. The terracotta figures were made by Joseph Nollekens in Rome and bought from him by the 9th Earl.

[130] Vista from the Fourth George Room through the Heaven Room to the Hell Staircase.

CHAPTER IV

— The Visit of Queen Victoria —

THERE WERE LONG LULLS IN ACTIVITY after the Elizabethan house was built by Lord Burghley and the 1st Earl of Exeter in the seventeenth century, and again after the baroque reconstruction of the interior by the 5th Earl and Countess in the late seventeenth. This was not to be the case in the early nineteenth century when the architectural momentum was maintained. The 9th Earl's nephew and successor, and the latter's eldest son in turn, carried on and completed the improvements culminating in lavish preparations for the visit of Queen Victoria to Burghley House in 1844. On that illustrious occasion the state rooms were finally brought into use for their historic purpose with the Queen and Prince Albert sleeping in the State Bedroom, the Second George Room. The royal visit was the culmination of the architectural development of the house over three centuries.

The 9th Earl had no children and was succeeded by his nephew Henry as 10th Earl (1754–1804) who seamlessly continued his predecessor's work and carried on the employment of Fell and Newton for furniture, overseeing the installation of the state bed in the Second George Room, enlarging the Capability Brown lake and expanding the park to the south-west by incorporating and planting an extensive new area enclosed by a long stone wall which creates an impressive impact for several miles alongside the Great North Road from London. The wall culminates in the Bottle Lodges which form a grand main entrance to the park on the edge of Stamford. The lodges were completed in 1801 and celebrated the 10th Earl of Exeter's promotion to marquess. This rise in rank was part of a consistent policy on the part of George III's Prime Minister, William Pitt the Younger, to reward and rally Tory supporters in the late Georgian period as the long 'Whig Supremacy' of the eighteenth century transmuted into Tory rule in the face of the French Revolution and its aftermath. The heads of several Tory families became marquesses around the same time including the other branch of the Cecils, the Earls of Salisbury at Hatfield House.

The Bottle Lodges took their cue from Lord Burghley's architecture and make a suitable overture to the house. A prominent triumphal arch in the centre sports Roman Doric columns like those of the lower stage of the east frontispiece in the central courtyard, and is linked by arches to flanking symmetrical lodges. They took the form of inflated versions of the ogee turrets on the west gatehouse and look like large bottles, hence the name immediately given to the gateway. Frilly top crestings with little obelisks and heraldry contribute to the Elizabethan spirit. It is a deliberate tribute to the panache and power of Lord Burghley's original design which has inspired all his successors to respect and emulate it down the centuries in the various additions to the place.

The lodges were built from 1799 to 1801; and the 10th Earl's promotion to marquess is proclaimed by the heraldry sporting his new coronet. They were designed by a local architect William Legg of Stamford (1743–1806). Born in London and trained as an architect there, Legg failed to be appointed to one of the three salaried district surveyor posts in the capital, so moved north and settled in Stamford as a surveyor and architect, a shrewd move. As well as work in the town including the market buildings (now demolished) he designed at various country houses in Lincolnshire and Northamptonshire. His Bottle Lodges at Burghley are a wonderfully lively composition and a remarkably early example of Elizabethan revival which only really took off in the 1830s. Legg was proud of the design and exhibited it at the Royal Academy in 1801. The gateway was a good advertisement for his talents on the busy Great North Road, as well as announcing the dynastic seat of a marquess.

The 1st Marquess finished his uncle's work to the George Rooms, as has been seen, employing James Newton of Fell and Newton until 1797 when Newton's final bill for £1,856.15s.9d was settled. Fell and Newton were also

[131] *previous pages* Burghley House from the park in early spring.

[132] *opposite* Sir Thomas Lawrence, *Portrait of Henry, 10th Earl and the 1st Marquess of Exeter, and his second wife Sarah with their daughter Sophia*. Known as the 'Cottage Countess', Sarah was the subject of a poem by Tennyson.

responsible for the professionally compiled inventory of contents drawn up in 1804 following the 1st Marquess's death. It throws light on the changes made to the house during the eleven years of his ownership which included some practical modernisation such as the installation of a water closet in the West Hall. (It is still there, with updated plumbing.) The completion and furnishing of the George Rooms allowed many of the grandest pieces of furniture and the largest Italian baroque paintings to be displayed in accordance with the 5th Earl's original intentions. The moving around of contents had an impact on the ground floor family rooms, especially those along the south front which were updated to meet Regency standards of comfort. The 1688 'Best Bedd Chamber', later the Turenne (Turin) Room at the west end now became the blue Drawing Room and was furnished by Newton. The floor was covered in Wilton carpet, and new furniture included a 'rosewood and gold bookcase' with a white marble top which is still there and a sofa and four elbow chairs.

In the seventeenth century there had been no floor carpets in the principal rooms and only a few in the eighteenth, but the 1st Marquess's furnishings included carpets in most rooms including Turkey carpets, Brussels Weave runners and needlework rugs. The original drawing room (the 'Blue Velvet Drawing Room' in 1738) now became the Red Drawing Room, the walls hung with red silk and extra furniture provided by Newton including three pier tables and matching glasses between the windows replacing the 8th Earl's 'sconces' by Phineas Evans. The James Newton pier glasses remain in this room today. The library on the north front was also made more comfortable with additional seat-furniture and a carpet. By the time of the 1st Marquess's death in 1804, not only had the George Rooms been completed in the grand European palace manner but the ground floor family apartments brought up to English late-Georgian standards of comfort which exceeded anything on the Continent and drew admiring comments from tourists to Britain. The bones of the 1st Marquess's arrangements are still detectable in the rooms today.

The key work of the 1st Marquess was the completion of the Great Stairs by commissioning murals for the upper wall to complement Verrio's ceiling. He employed Thomas Stothard (1755–1834), the painter and notable book illustrator who did a brilliant job in matching the ceiling with three new paintings framed between trompe *verde antico* Corinthian columns supporting the 5th Earl's painted cornice. The style of Stothard's work is not Italianate but more Rubensian with rich colouring. In 1797 the artist told Joseph Farington (secretary of the Royal Academy) that he had learnt much of Rubens's methods from Alexander Runciman (1736–1785), the Scottish painter who had trained in Rome and Naples and taught at the Royal Academy Schools when Stothard was studying there. Stothard's work on the staircase walls comprises three large scenes: that on the north wall shows a very Rubensian banquet indicative of 'Intemperance'; the west wall shows the descent of Orpheus into the Underworld; the east wall depicts the Horrors of War. Presumably these subjects were chosen to relate to Verrio's 'Hell'.

The painter was left alone to concentrate on his work—very much the lone genius. Stothard described his working method at Burghley to Farington who recorded it in his diary: 'He has an apartment where he breakfasts and dines seeing the family only occasionally. He is deaf and mixed society cannot amuse him. Works about 6 hours daily. Lord Exeter does not interfere. Much pleased with Lady Exeter (late Dowager Duchess of Hamilton) who appears to conduct herself in a very domestic and proper manner, paying great attention to his Lordship's children by a former wife.' This suggests that Stothard was given a free hand and was treated sensitively. He certainly rose to the occasion and produced one of his major artistic works.

The 1st Marquess did not collect Italian paintings like his predecessors but was a major patron of Sir Thomas Lawrence (1769–1830), the most accomplished portraitist of the day. The paintings he commissioned of the family included full lengths of Lord Exeter with his second wife, Sarah Hoggins, and their young daughter Sophia, and one of his third wife, the dowager duchess, for which Newton provided the gilt frame. There is no portrait of Lord Exeter's first wife, Emma Vernon of Hanbury Hall, Worcestershire, and their marriage ended in acrimony when she left him for the curate, the Revd. William Sneyd in 1789. In retaliation he extirpated all traces of her from his life and sold the contents of her family house, Hanbury Hall, where they had lived while his uncle was alive, to pay the Vernon estate debts. As they broke up before Henry Cecil's inheritance, Emma Vernon never lived at Burghley. He divorced her by Act of Parliament (then the only means of obtaining a divorce) in 1791, after which she married her 'consumptive curate' and the couple went to live in Portugal.

After the breakdown of his first marriage Henry Cecil lodged with a Shropshire farmer called Hoggins under the assumed name of 'John Jones', pretending to be an artist. He may have had some painterly talent as his daughter Lady Sophia Cecil certainly was a competent amateur artist who made a series of drawings of the interiors at Burghley which show the rooms in their Regency guise. Henry fell in love with Sarah, the daughter of his landlord, and married her. They had three children, but she died of puerperal problems after the third, when she was only twenty-three. Tennyson was inspired to write his poem 'The Lord of Burleigh' about the tragedy:

[133] *opposite & below* Lady Sophia Cecil, *Engravings after Drawings of the Fourth George Room and Dining Room*, with the lava table in situ and a buffet display of gold and silver plate on the sideboard and the Rollos silver cistern.

So she droop'd before him
Fading slowly from his side
Three fair children first she bore him,
Then before her time she died.

The 'Cottage Countess' became part of the Burghley story, adding a sad romantic tinge. After Sarah's death, the 1st Marquess married more conventionally the widowed Duchess of Hamilton, but it was Sarah's son Brownlow (1795–1867) who succeeded his father as 2nd Marquess and completed the architectural embellishment.

The 2nd Marquess's most important change at Burghley was the construction of corridors round all four sides of the Lord Treasurer's inner court at ground level, and part of the first floor level. This overcame the impracticality of enfilades of rooms only reached by progressing through

all of them, and the family rooms to north and south not being directly accessible from each side of the court under cover. This addition impaired the original proportions of the Elizabethan court but the work was done tactfully. Attempts had already been made to solve the access problems including the construction of greenhouse-like glazed links between the sides, giving a direct covered cruciform way between all sides of the court. This eccentric but useful makeshift arrangement spoilt the appearance of the courtyard. The 2nd Marquess's solution was preferable on architectural and practical grounds. The new corridors enhanced the privacy and convenience of the rooms. They also gave separate circulation for servants reflecting modern domestic planning. In the eighteenth century and earlier everyone had lived close together. The 9th Earl referred to the household as 'his family' but by the Victorian age, staff and family lived more segregated lives.

Corridors had already been added to other houses in the early nineteenth century, for instance at Longleat and Chatsworth by Jeffry Wyatville or the gothic cloisters above service corridors by James Wyatt at Wilton. So the 2nd Marquess was in step with advances in contemporary house planning as well as completing his father's intention of making the ground floor a comfortable and convenient modern residence. The corridors added a new architectural feature, exciting in its own right. Pevsner described them as an 'exciting piece of Elizabethan-style scenery'.

The architect chosen for this new addition was John Gandy Deering (1787–1850) and the work was carried out from 1824 to 1828. Gandy Deering was a sophisticated and scholarly designer who came from an architectural family, his two brothers also being architects. All three were pupils of James Wyatt, an occurrence owed to Wyatt's design for Whites in St. James's where their father worked as the club porter. When Wyatt designed the new club house there in 1787 he was struck by the ability as a draughtsman of Joseph Gandy, the porter's eldest son, and took him into his office, and then employed the two younger brothers John and Michael who also showed artistic ability. John trained at the Royal Academy Schools winning the silver medal and then travelled under the sponsorship of the Society of Dilettanti to Greece and Asia in the company of the Graecophile Sir William Gell, publishing the *Unedited Antiquities of Attica* in 1817. His design work is mainly in a polished neo-classical manner but like all good Regency architects he could handle most styles, and obviously relished pulling out all the Elizabethan stops for the corridors at Burghley. It was not his only job for Lord Exeter, as he also designed the 'Tudor' Infirmary at Stamford and the new Exeter Exchange in London as part of the Strand Improvements when the leases of that property came up for renewal again in 1830. By that stage Gandy had retired from the architectural profession on inheriting the Deering estate in Buckinghamshire and changing his name. He transmuted into a country

[134] *opposite left* Pietra dura casket from the collection of William Beckford. Acquired at the Fonthill sale by the 2nd Marquess in 1823.

[135] *opposite right* Miniature by Isaac Oliver of the Browne family, Viscounts Montague of Cowdray Park, inherited by the wife of the 2nd Marquess.

[136] *below* The Walsingham Bowl. Chinese porcelain of c. 1580, with European silver-gilt mounts. Reputedly a present from Elizabeth I to Sir Thomas Walsingham.

gentleman, becoming High Sheriff of Buckinghamshire and MP for Aylesbury. He is a good example of Georgian social mobility, from club servant to 'landed gent' in two generations. The corridors at Burghley showed the architectural talent that was not to be developed further as a result of his cutting short his professional career. He was proud of them and exhibited his designs for Burghley at the Royal Academy, just as Legg had done with the Bottle Lodges, and it was on the strength of the corridor designs that he was elected to the Royal Academy.

An interesting development at Burghley in the early nineteenth century was its emergence as a national showplace: one of the greatest monuments of Elizabethan architecture. It came to be visited by thousands of paying visitors every year, partly because of its prominent location on the Great North Road, and was celebrated in patriotic terms in the afterglow of defeat of the French revolutionaries and Napoleon. The 9th Earl had opened the house on a regular basis as part of his Enlightenment philanthropic and educational outlook. The pioneer of Picturesque tours, William Gilpin in 1771 had declared: 'Burghley House is one of the noblest monuments of British architecture in the reign of Queen Elizabeth'. This view gathered strength in the time of the 1st and 2nd Marquesses. Printed guidebooks to the place set the tone, and this partly explains the fostering of the Elizabethan aura in the early nineteenth century. *The History or Description . . . of Burghley House* published by John Horn in Stamford in 1797 described the house as 'so long the admiration of taste', and added that such a monument to the 'free and commercial kingdom of Great Britain' was admired by foreigners as well as English visitors. Thomas Blore's *Guide to Burghley House* in 1815 likewise praised it as a 'palace', a 'baronial habitation' and a 'magnificent pile'. The architecture was redolent of the achievement of its 'illustrious founder' to whom England 'owes much perhaps of her present grandeur and security'.

It was not just tourists who visited Burghley. The 2nd Marquess was a considerable host and gave large house parties, a manifestation of the uncontrolled personal extravagance which would once again imperil the family finances, though the 2nd Marquess had married another heiress, Isabel Poyntz of Cowdray Park who brought further works of art including important miniatures. The 2nd Marquess also bought Beckford objects from the Fonthill Abbey sale and Venetian chairs from the Doge's Palace. Queen Victoria visited Burghley House twice; the first time as a young princess with her mother the Duchess of Kent in 1835. The little travelling tent bed in which she slept on that occasion is still in place in the Brown Drawing Room. Queen Adelaide, the widow of William IV, came to stay in 1842. The Great Occasion, however, was the three-day visit of Queen Victoria with her new husband Prince Albert of Saxe-Coburg-Gotha in November 1844. This was one of a series of visits to her 'principal subjects', the owners of the great country houses, to introduce Prince Albert to England and to foster relations between the people and their sovereign, enabling the Queen

[137] *opposite* Watercolour of the Second George Room (State Bedroom) as prepared for the visit of Queen Victoria in 1844.

to be seen in different parts of the country by taking advantage of the newly constructed railways. The idea behind these visits was that of Sir Robert Peel, the Prime Minister. The royal tours in the 1840s were in the way of state visits, and had an important political dimension, to cement relations between the crown and country. Peel's far-sighted policies, including making the monarchy popular and the repeal of the Corn Laws, thereby ensuring cheaper food, were the reason why England was the only European country not engulfed by the revolutions of 1848. (The Chartist riots were a damp squib.)

Other houses visited by the Queen and Prince Albert were Arundel Castle in Sussex, Castle Howard in Yorkshire, Chatsworth in Derbyshire, Hatfield House in Hertfordshire, Stowe in Buckinghamshire, Woburn Abbey in Bedfordshire, and Dalkeith Palace and Taymouth Castle in Scotland. The prospective hosts were given up to two years notice to prepare their houses for the visitation. In the case of the Duke of Buckingham it was his extravagance in refurbishing Stowe and the costs of the royal entertainment that tipped him into bankruptcy, leading to the sale of the contents of Stowe in 1848. Lord Exeter was commendably energetic, and the preparations for the Queen's visit were the main focus for his improvements at Burghley. He restored the Great Hall, intended as the setting for the banquet and ball, refitted and modernised the kitchen, re-furnished the state bedroom, and embellished the chapel which was to be used for the christening of Lord Exeter's daughter in the presence of the Queen with Prince Albert as sponsor. (The Prince naturally suggested the name Victoria for his Cecil godchild.) All these works were directly instigated by the royal visit.

The main thrust of the 2nd Marquess's effort was directed at the east range with the kitchen, hall and chapel. The kitchen had remained for three centuries as built by Lord Burghley, but was refitted in 1841 to 1842 to include all the latest in modern technology including new cast iron coal-fired cooking ranges and ovens and steam-heated warming cupboards, all provided by Benham and Sons of Wigmore Street, London. This equipment was modelled on the pioneering new kitchen at the Reform Club in London, fitted out in 1841 under the direction of the famous chef Alexis Soyer (1810–1858), which also used Benham stoves and equipment. Since the 5th Earl's time, the Great Hall which had been a deliberate medieval throw-back on Lord Burghley's part, had not played a major role in the house and seems to have been largely disused in the eighteenth century. The 1st Marquess converted it into a museum for a collection of eighty glass-fronted cases of stuffed British birds bought from Lieutenant Bell in Yorkshire in 1801. These were moved to the garden temple where they later fell victim to damp and insects. The popular revival of interest in 'Olden Time', fanned by the novels of Walter Scott, George IV's 'Tudor' coronation, and Joseph Nash's lithographic illustrations of ancient 'mansions' published from 1839 onwards, inspired the 2nd Marquess to refurbish the Great Hall for the splendid entertainment he planned for Queen Victoria.

The Burghley Great Hall was repaired between 1838 and 1842 in the spirit of the Lord Treasurer's creation, respecting the hammerbeam roof and the 1573 Serlian chimneypiece, but otherwise refitted and redecorated. The lower parts of the walls were lined with antiquarian oak joinery, incorporating bookcases, and a minstrels' gallery was inserted at the north end, the work of the estate joiner, Mr. Smith. The windows were filled with ancient glass and modern heraldry in 1838, under the direction of Thomas Willement (1786–1871), who was 'Artist in Stained Glass to Queen Victoria', a reviver of the medieval craft, and one of the leading antiquarians of the time. The Willement windows incorporated some of the splendid fifteenth-century glass from Tattershall church in Lincolnshire which had been bought by the 9th Earl to save it in 1757. The majority had been installed in St. Martin's Church, Stamford by William

[138] *below* Medieval stained glass from Tattershall church, inserted in the Great Hall windows in 1838 by the 2nd Marquess under the direction of Thomas Willement.

[139] *opposite* Henry Bryan Ziegler, *The Great Hall during the banquet given by the 2nd Marquess for Queen Victoria in 1844*. Lord Exeter restored the room to the glory of 'Old England' especially for this.

Peckitt of York, the leading Georgian glass specialist, one window given to Warwick Castle, and some intended for the chapel at Burghley. It was the latter which was installed in the Great Hall windows.

The stained glass was not the only antiquarian material re-used in Lord Exeter's scheme. The lower wall joinery incorporated Flemish baroque woodwork from Tongerlo Abbey in modern Belgium, which had been closed and looted by French Revolutionary forces in 1796. Though the abbey was revived in 1840, many fittings which had been removed were sold in London through the antiquarian dealers based around Wardour Street who gave their name to this type of recycled Flemish woodwork. The joinery reused at Burghley was probably part of the choir stalls including carved panels and Salomonic columns from the abbey church. (The present Gothic revival church at Tongerlo was built in the 1850s.) The refitting of the Hall was completed by the installation of bronze gothic Colza oil chandeliers hanging from the hammerbeams. They were bought from Hardenberg of Mount Street, London, specialists in decorative light fittings, who also provided the 1st Marquess with the Vestal Virgins in bronzed plaster holding lamps for the chapel in 1801. The upgrading of the purlieus of the Great Hall included the creation of a purpose-built fire-proof muniment room with unique black iron record cabinets sporting the embossed gilt Exeter arms on their doors. These were supplied by Chubb, the safe specialists.

Upstairs in the east range, the 2nd Marquess embellished the Chapel and Ante Chapel, retaining Capability Brown's 'Elizabethan' ceilings and inserting a huge marble

and scagliola chimneypiece against the north wall. This is Portuguese baroque with polychrome Salomonic columns and a central shell-headed niche. It looks disconcertingly like an altarpiece and rather overshadows the more modest Anglican Communion table against the east wall, or would do if it were not for the large Veronese altar painting hung above the latter by the 9th Earl. This ornate scagliola eye-catcher came from a 'convent near Lisbon' and was acquired by the 2nd Marquess through the good offices of the 6th Lord Howard de Walden who was British envoy to the Kingdom of Portugal in the 1830s and 1840s. It is very much in the spirit of the 5th Earl and Countess's baroque taste and complements the carved oak swags and pendants by Maine and Young which with their winged cherubs' heads were obviously made for the Chapel on the inspiration of those by Grinling Gibbons in Charles II's chapel at Windsor Castle, now dismantled.

While the 2nd Marquess's improvements in preparation for the Queen's visit were largely targeted on the east wing, he could not resist ornamenting the lily, and further enhancing the George Rooms so recently completed by his father and great uncle. He added the exceptional silver mounts to the fire grates, and gilded the seat-furniture, commissioning new white and gold items for the bedroom from the fashionable London furnishers George Morant and Son. This must have given the Queen a slight feeling of déjà vu, for several other of her hosts in the 1840s also commissioned Morant furniture especially for their royal visits, including a new state bed at Arundel. At Burghley the 1795 Fell and Newton bed was retained in the Second George Room but adapted to make it more usable, the pedestals and dais being removed and new, simpler hangings substituted. By 1844 Burghley was ready for the Royal Visit which had been anticipated in its architecture for the best part of three

centuries. The Queen used the Third George Room as her sitting room, and the Fourth George as her breakfast room.

Lord Exeter had good reason to be satisfied by the results of all his efforts, and by the appreciative contemporary coverage of the 'Princely Hospitality of Burghley'.[11] Everything went to plan except of course the weather. It was grey, wet, and drizzly. The Queen and Prince Albert and their Household travelled by special train of four carriages from Euston to Weedon near Northampton on Tuesday, 12 November 1844. The Royal Party left London at twenty-two minutes past nine, with the Royal Standard flying from the engine and a gilded crown on top of the royal coach. The train sped along at thirty-five miles an hour with a stop at Tring to take in water for the engine, and reached Weedon, a small station on the main west coast line, as planned at fifteen minutes to twelve. Along the route many trackside spectators waved and cheered including, it was noted, workmen in ordinary clothes and neckerchiefs. From Weedon a procession set off for Northampton, the carriages and horses having been brought from the Royal Mews on an earlier train and standing ready, formed up. At Weedon the Queen was met by Lord Exeter as Lord Lieutenant, the High Sheriff of Northamptonshire Sir Henry Dryden, the Justices of the Peace, and a Guard of Honour of the 47th Regiment Queen's Colour. At Northampton the Queen was met by the Mayor and civic dignitaries, and massed school children, and given luncheon in the Guild Hall.

Meanwhile Lord Exeter rode back at speed to Stamford, ready to be there to greet The Queen again, as Lord of Burghley. A 'splendid arch' designed by 'his Lordship's architect' was erected over the road at Duddington to mark the 'beginning of Lord Exeter's property'. Crowds lined the last five miles to Stamford which was decked with flags and 'Long Live The Queen' banners. The Royal Party was received by the Mayor and Corporation of Stamford, and Lord Exeter gave a dinner at the George Inn for 150 of his 'chief tenants' who had formed a greeting party. By this time the drizzle had turned to heavy rain. The Queen arrived at 'the stately towers' of Burghley at four thirty and was taken by Lady Exeter to the George Rooms to rest. The banquet in the Great Hall took place at eight o'clock under the light of the ten new chandeliers, and there was a magnificent buffet of gold plate and silver arranged in the bay window including the Rollos wine cooler and the Lord High Almoner's perquisite dishes accumulated from generations of coronations. The party comprised the Cecil family, the Royal Household,

[140] Henry Bryan Ziegler, watercolour of Queen Victoria and Prince Albert planting an oak and a lime tree in the grounds of Burghley House during her visit in 1844.

the Dukes of Rutland and Bedford, the Marquess of Northampton, other local families and Sir Robert Peel, the Prime Minister. The band of the Coldstream Guards (which had also come by train) played in the minstrels' gallery, and all the footmen wore new Exeter state livery of blue and silver. The scene was captured in a watercolour by Henry Bryan Ziegler (1798–1874) who was hired by Lord Exeter to make a series of views to record the visit.

The following day was too wet to go out, so was devoted to looking at the house and collections. The Queen even visited the kitchen, and she and Prince Albert took a particular interest in the paintings which paralleled the Royal Collection, then in the process of redisplay at Windsor and Buckingham Palace under Prince Albert's direction. The baptism of Lady Victoria Cecil by the Bishop of Peterborough took place in the Chapel in the evening, and was attended by the Queen. Prince Albert gave a gold christening cup to his god-daughter, inscribed 'To Lady Victoria Cecil. From Her Godfather Albert. Burghley. November 13th 1844'. At dinner that evening, a different group of guests were invited, including the Marquess and Marchioness of Salisbury (of the other Cecil branch), the Bishop of Peterborough and his wife, and the Earl of Gainsborough and his wife. The rain abated slightly, and the fireworks took place as planned with Capability Brown's bridge 'tastefully and brilliantly' illuminated as the backdrop.

On Thursday morning the rain stopped and the weather turned fine. The men went out shooting in the morning, and the Royal Visit to Stamford, including a look at the ruins of Jacobean Wothorpe, took place in the dry, and the tree planting went ahead in the afternoon using special spades (though a lighter child's spade had to be substituted for the Queen). Prince Albert planted an oak and Queen Victoria a lime. Dinner that evening was attended by other neighbouring Northamptonshire grandees including Earl Fitzwilliam and Lord Lilford and their spouses. A Dress Ball followed in the Great Hall beginning at nine thirty and was attended by five hundred guests. The Royal Household and the men wore court or military uniform, and the women sparkled in 'brilliant gems'. Queen Victoria and Prince Albert departed at nine-thirty on Friday morning. The 2nd Marquess subsequently became an active courtier, serving briefly as Lord Steward of the Household, and was appointed ADC to The Queen, and created a Knight of the Garter.

Lord Exeter lived on in a semi-regal glow at Burghley for a further twenty-three years but did no more to the house after the considerable expenditure of his first four decades. On his death in 1867 after sixty-three years as owner of Burghley, he bequeathed a glorious house and an encumbered estate to his eldest son and successor William, 3rd Marquess of Exeter (1825–1895). He, too, continued to live extravagantly, with race horses, yachts, and long visits to the Riviera where he was a regular at the gaming tables of Biarritz and Monte Carlo. The 3rd Marquess concentrated more on the agricultural estate, breeding shorthorn cattle and experimenting with fish farming, importing black bass from Canada as a commercial venture. He also spent a fortune on horses and racing. He owned several yachts, another expensive hobby. Combined with the previous heavy outlay on building and furnishing, the yachts and horses landed the property once more with heavy debts.

Like other aristocratic landowners who, thanks to geography, had not benefitted latterly from the manufacturing, mineral and urban wealth of the Industrial Revolution, and who had built up high levels of estate debt, the 3rd Marquess was badly affected by the agricultural depression after 1870. The economic decline of British farming lasted for seventy years and was caused by the first wave of 'Globalisation' with the import of cheap food into England from abroad after the building of railways in North and South America and the British colonies around the world, and the invention of refrigerated ships. This enabled cheap corn to be imported

[141] *below left* The 3rd Marquess's steam yacht, one of the extravagances that contributed to an economic debacle and estate sales in the late-nineteenth century.

[142] *below right* 'Stockwell', one of the 2nd Marquess's racehorses. Racing was another of the family's financial extravagances.

[143] *opposite* The 3rd Marquess's Shorthorn Prize Cattle, bred at the home farm. He also tried fish farming as a commercial venture, which added to the estate debts.

from Canada and the United States, beef from Argentina, mutton and wool from Australia and New Zealand, and even eggs from China, and undercut home production. The impact on British farming was disastrous, leading to drastic reductions in farm incomes and rentals, and collapsing land values. This economic decline reduced the income from the Burghley estate and meant there was no money for further architectural improvement in the second half of the nineteenth century, nor was there going to be for the ensuing hundred years. In some ways this was beneficial as it allowed the cumulative Elizabethan, Stuart and Georgian achievement in the house to survive intact, without Victorian or twentieth-century alteration. Relative poverty is the greatest preserver of 'heritage', as attested by the survival of baroque Rome thanks to the bankruptcy of the eighteenth-century Papacy, Venice due to the collapse of its commercial trading empire, or medieval East Anglia and the Cotswolds because textile manufacturing moved to the industrial north of England after the 1760s.

The 3rd Marquess had no option but to sell parts of the estate. Many thousands of acres were disposed of including the Fen land with the best farming soil in England and the Exeter Exchange urban property in London, both of which would have been extremely valuable and useful assets had they still been held in the twenty-first century. To some extent, this attrition was peripheral, and enough remained to maintain the house which continued to be open to the public in the summer, being visited by four thousand paying visitors annually in the last decades of the nineteenth century, which was remarkable bearing in mind its remoteness from large centres of population and the big cities. Only Chatsworth and Warwick Castle had more visitors and the former was situated mid-way between Manchester and Sheffield, and the latter was near Birmingham, three of the biggest boom towns of the nineteenth century. The 3rd Marquess was able to keep the place in good order, and even to modernise the domestic side. As soon as he inherited he installed gas light with a gasworks built on

the estate. A notebook kept by him recorded that 706,920 cubic feet of gas were produced a year. A second gas holder to contain eight thousand cubic feet was erected in 1870. The light fittings in the house included adaptations of old chandeliers, like those in the Great Hall, and additional decorative brackets and candelabra. The gas supplied one thousand lights of which seven hundred were in the house and stables.

This project was, however, undertaken before the impact of agricultural recession became apparent, and seriously dented the estate rental income. When it did in the course of the later 1870s, there was a very serious threat to Burghley and other historic houses. In 1882 Parliament, in response to the crisis facing the landed interest, passed the Settled Land Act. This legislation relaxed the laws of entail and enabled historic chattels to be sold by the life-tenants. The art collection at Burghley had been entailed with the estate and title by the 5th Earl, and the entail had been maintained by his successors. Now the 3rd Marquess had the power to sell 'settled chattels' including paintings, silver and porcelain. The inevitable sale took place at Christie's in June 1888. It was not as disastrous as it might have been, mainly because the sort of Italian *Seicento* art collected by the 5th Earl, which is the special glory of the collection, was then the nadir of fashion. Late nineteenth-century collectors preferred early Italian art and the High Renaissance. Christie's advised that most of the collection was of no commercial value, so it all stayed on the walls. Only thirty paintings were sold and they were the 9th Earl's geese masquerading as swans still in the 1880s attributed to Rubens, Dürer, Van Eyck, Velasquez, Leonardo and Titian. Thanks to the 'optimistic' attributions and provenances of the Roman *ciceroni* Byres and Jenkins, these doubtful 'stars' saved the collection in 1888, though none of them have since stood up to modern scholarship. Timing is everything, and the 5th Earl and Countess's unique collection survived the 1880s financial crisis intact.

[144] Detail of the west entrance in the Courtyard passages, designed by John Gandy Deering for the 2nd Marquess of Exeter in 1824–28.

The 3rd Marquess died after a long and extravagant reign in 1895, being succeeded briefly as 4th Marquess by his son, another Brownlow (1849–1898). He had sat as MP for South Lincolnshire in his father's lifetime and was a member of the Privy Council. In 1891 he had been appointed Vice Chamberlain of the Royal Household, continuing his father's connection with Queen Victoria's court. He married Isabella, only daughter and heiress of Sir Thomas Whichcote of Aswarby Park, Lincolnshire. She brought to Burghley the two beautiful portraits by Thomas Gainsborough of her ancestors Sir Christopher and Lady Whichcote. They complemented the fine works by Angelica Kauffman and Lawrence already in the collection. The 4th Marquess only outlived his father by three years, dying in 1898. On his death the estate was subject to death duties for the first time since the creation of the new tax in Lord Harcourt's Liberal Budget in 1894, though the tax rate was not as high as it became in the twentieth century when it gradually rose to 80 percent of the value of an estate after the Second World War. Works of art of national importance were exempted from the tax from the start to protect historic collections from dispersal. Although to some extent in practice paintings have often been sold to pay the tax on other property. Again Burghley was lucky, just as it had been when the 5th Earl's collection was deemed valueless at the time of the 1888 sale, in that William the 5th Marquess (1876–1956) lived for over sixty years after inheriting, avoiding death duties during the first half of the twentieth century when taxes in Britain were raised exponentially to pay for two World Wars and to create a state system of social provision. The 5th Marquess was a remarkable man who devoted his life to preserving Burghley, its art collection and keeping the estate together during challenging war time conditions. He rode out the continuing agricultural depression up to 1939 when British farming was belatedly protected to provide food during the Second World War, a policy continued by governments after the war leading to an agricultural boom from the 1950s onwards. He even bought additional land. He was active in public service as Lord Lieutenant of Northamptonshire from 1922 to 1951, Mayor of Stamford and many other local roles. He was also ADC to King George V, and was created a Knight of the Garter as the 2nd Marquess had been, and the 1st Earl in the seventeenth century, as well as the great Lord Burghley himself in the reign of Queen Elizabeth I. He married the Hon. Myra Orde-Powlett (1879–1973), daughter of the 5th Lord Bolton. Together they protected Burghley through very difficult times, and Lady Exeter was particularly interested in the art collections, rearranging the paintings, doing research in the archives and producing a privately printed catalogue of the pictures in 1954 which is still the basis for understanding the collection today.

During the First World War the house was used as a hospital for wounded soldiers. In the Second World War a bomb fell in the park and the resulting explosion broke all the window panes on the north and west fronts. Generally, however, the place escaped lightly and survived to be reopened to the public in 1946, one of the first houses to do so after the war. By then the house had become shabby and in need of repair and modernisation. No decoration had been done since before the First World War. Lord and Lady Exeter were essentially Victorians, and the house remained totally unmodernised, even still lit by gas, which over the years gradually darkened all the paintings, especially Verrio's murals. With the passing of time, the old textiles fell into disrepair and were hanging in tatters by the 1960s. Like most English country houses after the Second World War, Burghley was kept going on a proverbial shoe string, but thanks to Lord and Lady Exeter's devotion and care, it survived intact into the later twentieth century when changes in the law and taxation made it possible to establish an independent trust to secure the permanent preservation of the house, park and the collections for posterity.

[145] West and north sides of the courtyard, with the passages added to improve circulation by the 2nd Marquess, and which rise to the occasion architecturally with a rare combination of tact and panache.

[146] *left & right*
John Gandy Deering's architectural detail carefully matched the Elizabethan architecture.

[147] The interior of John Gandy Deering's north passage, light and practical, with elegant ribbed stucco ceilings.

[148] The Blue Drawing Room refurnished by Fell and Newton, part of a Regency campaign to make the family rooms more comfortable.

[149] The Brown Drawing Room. The Gainsborough portraits of Lady Whichcote and her husband Sir Thomas Whichcote were inherited by the wife of the 4th Marquess.

[150] The Brown Drawing Room. The red silk–hung tent bed was prepared for the young Princess Victoria on her visit to Burghley with her mother in 1835.

[151] The Second George Room as prepared for Queen Victoria's visit in 1844.

[152] Bed steps used by Queen Victoria.

[153] Dressing table by George Morant, the fashionable London furnisher.

[154] Garden spades. The smaller one was used by Queen Victoria for the royal tree planting ceremony at Burghley in 1844, the larger ones were made by the estate carpenter for Queen Elizabeth II and Prince Philip in 2012.

[155] *left & right* Thomas Stothard's murals on the walls of the Hell Staircase, 1800. They depict 'Intemperance', 'The Descent of Orpheus into the Underworld', and 'Horrors of Wars'—subjects thought to be analogous to Hell.

[156] The Chapel with bronzed plaster vestals holding lamps by Hardenberg of London, acquired by the 1st Marquess *c.* 1801.

[157] *left & right*
The Chapel with Portuguese marble chimneypiece, grander than the altar, brought from Lisbon by the 2nd Marquess.

[158] The Kitchen stoves. The height of modern technology, these were supplied by Benham and Sons in 1841–42. They also fitted the kitchen of Barry's new Reform Club in Pall Mall, London.

[159] The Kitchen dresser, with part of the nineteenth-century copper *batterie de cuisine*. Queen Victoria inspected the kitchen as part of her tour of the house during her stay at Burghley.

BLUE DRAWING RM
GREEN DAMASK BEDROOM
LADY EXETER'S DRESSING RM
QUEEN ELIZABETH'S BEDROOM
PAGODA ROOM
PURPLE SATIN BEDROOM
PURPLE SATIN DRESSING RM
1ST GEORGE ROOM
2ND GEORGE ROOM
3RD GEORGE ROOM
4TH GEORGE ROOM
BLACK & YELLOW BEDROOM
BROWN DRAWING RM
GREEN VELVET DRESSING RM
CRIMSON VELVET BEDROOM
1 - WEST GALLERY
4 - WEST GALLERY
GREEN DAMASK DRESSING RM
OLD BLUE BEDROOM
LADIES' MAIDS CALL-BELL
6 - WEST GALLERY
5 WEST GALLERY
2 - WEST GALLERY
3 - WEST GALLERY

[160] The servants' bells giving the names of the rooms in the nineteenth century.

[161] Fire buckets in the Hog's Hall by the back door. In the eighteenth century, there was also a fire engine kept in the Great Hall, part of a system of fire precautions.

10 BOX
11 BOX
12 BOX
13 BOX
14 BOX
15 BOX
16 BOX
17 BOX
18 BOX

[162] *left & right* The Muniments Room, with Chubb iron patent safes for fire-proof preservation of the archives. The doors carry gilt examples of the Exeter arms.

[163] The Great Hall with reused seventeenth-century woodwork from the abbey of Tongerlo in modern Belgium, which had been displaced by French Revolutionary forces in 1796.

[164] The Great Hall, restored by the 2nd Marquess in 1838–42 after a long period of disuse.

[165] The Great Hall, with heraldic glass in the windows made by Thomas Willement to complement the medieval glass which was also incorporated there.

[166] The Bottle Lodges, built for the 1st Marquess in 1801 and celebrating his promotion in the peerage to serve as the main entrance to the park. They were designed by the Stamford architect William Legg and form a creditable homage to the architecture of the main house.

CHAPTER V

— Burghley in the Modern Era —

THE REVIVAL OF BURGHLEY HOUSE IN the later twentieth century has been one of the most significant recent English restoration successes thanks to the strategic foresight of the 6th Marquess of Exeter and the dynamism of his daughter and granddaughter in continuing his vision, with the support of the trust which he established. The story of English country houses and the landed families which created and own them in the second half of the twentieth century is often spun as one of ruin and terminal decline but it is more complex, nuanced and interesting than that. Some houses were demolished and some families declined—they always have—but others have seen a renaissance. It could be argued that generally both the places and their owners enjoyed a renewed lease of life in the sixty years after the Second World War. The listing of historic buildings in the 1947 Planning Act, the establishment of the grant-giving Historic Buildings Council and its successors, following the Gowers Report commissioned by the post-war Labour Chancellor of the Exchequer, and the development of commercial opening to the public in the 1950s, catering for the rapid spread of car ownership and resulting home tourism, gave additional purpose and financial support to houses, some of which like Burghley had been open to visitors for a long time but now became more professional with tea rooms, guidebooks and other facilities, transforming themselves into businesses in their own right.

The revival of the country house and the beginning of a national system of preservation of landscape and buildings in the 1940s and 1950s was very much the result of policies initiated by Clement Attlee's post-war Labour government which realised that 'national heritage' mattered, and that grants for owners and protection for buildings were the fair and civilized concomitant to high taxes for social welfare, if historic places were to survive. A further significant boost to the 'national heritage' (that is, privately owned historic buildings and landscape) came from the Labour governments of the late 1960s and early 1970s with the Civic Amenities Act in 1967, which strengthened protection for listed buildings and established conservation areas, and then the 1976 Finance Act introduced by Denis Healey when Chancellor of the Exchequer. This latter legislation enabled independent charitable trusts specifically for the preservation of historic buildings and landscapes, which hitherto had been impossible except under the cloak of educational, religious or medical purposes. The 1976 Act also allowed the establishment of historic buildings maintenance funds. This was a game-changer, and within twenty-five years nearly all the most significant and largest privately owned country houses in England were vested in charitable preservation trusts such as Arundel Castle, Chatsworth, Grimsthorpe, Harewood or Wilton. Burghley was one of the pioneers. Lord Exeter with the help of his lawyers, Farrers, had been planning along similar lines for some years previously and had set up the Burghley House Preservation Trust in 1969 which could therefore take immediate advantage of the new preservation framework established by the 1976 Act. Burghley was a pioneer of dedicated trusts to preserve historic houses and collections. A significant proportion of the surrounding estate, including farms, woods and commercial and domestic property, was transferred as an endowment for the new trust.

The 6th Marquess (1905–1981) was a remarkable man, and in some ways his life epitomised the twentieth-century renewal of the role of the old landed families, being the first member of the family since the early seventeenth century to play a significant part in national, as opposed to local, affairs. At Eton and Magdalene College, Cambridge he excelled as a sportsman and athlete and continued to be active in those fields. In the lifetime of his father he was known by his courtesy title of Lord Burghley. Under that soubriquet he earned an international reputation as

[167] *previous pages* The lake and boathouse.

[168] *left* Burghley in use as a hospital during the First World War. Capability Brown's orangery was a hospital ward.

a hurdler between 1924 and 1933, winning the Athletics Association 120 Yards Hurdles Championship in 1929, 1930, and 1931; the 440 Yards Hurdles title in 1926, 1927, 1928, 1930, and 1932. In 1927 he established (briefly) a new world record of 54.2 seconds. His victory in the 1928 Olympics 400 metres hurdles in Amsterdam, where he won the gold medal, made him internationally famous. He also won the silver medal in the 1932 Olympics in Los Angeles. In 1932 and 1936 he was British Olympics Captain in the games held in the United States and Germany. On the strength of his own achievement he was an enthusiastic promoter of amateur sport. After the Second World War he became President of the Amateur Athletics Association, the International Amateur Athletics Federation and a member of the International Olympic Committee. In 1948 he was Chairman of the Organising and Executive Committee of the London Olympic Games, held that year following a twelve year hiatus caused by World War II. It was the second time London had hosted the Olympic Games, having done so previously in 1908. Known as the 'Austerity Games', Lord Burghley and his team's arrangements in 1948 were achieved within a tight budget, and re-used the existing Wembley Stadium built for the Empire Exhibition in 1924. It was thanks to Lord Burghley (with the backing of George VI) that the games, which had been awarded to London in 1939, went ahead despite financial misgivings in certain quarters, after he personally went to see the Chairman of the Olympics Committee in Stockholm to convince him London could do it. War-time army and RAF camps were used to house the athletes rather than expensive new-built 'Olympic villages', including one in Richmond Park where Lord Burghley unfurled the Olympic Flag to mark the opening in July 1948. The main opening ceremony attended by King George VI, Queen Elizabeth, and the Dowager Queen Mary, took place at Wembley on 26 July where the Royal party was welcomed by Lord Burghley: 'A visionary dream has today become a glorious reality.'

The sort of experience gained in organising the Olympics against a backdrop of rationing and post-war retrenchment stood Lord Burghley in good stead when in due course he came to tackle the future of his great inheritance at Burghley in the context of continuing economic difficulties, though rationing was finally phased out in the year he succeeded his father. Nor was the honing of his organisational skills and strategic vision restricted to sporting events. He had also had a hand in running countries. From 1943 to 1945 he served as Governor and Commander-in-Chief of Bermuda, a British Overseas Territory in the Atlantic Ocean since 1612, with a massive Royal Naval Dockyard, then the biggest in the western hemisphere. It was of great strategic importance during the war. When his father died aged eighty in 1956, after an exceptionally long time in charge at Burghley, therefore, he had a considerable hinterland that would be useful in tackling Burghley and planning a long-term future for the house and estate. One fruit of this was the establishment of the Burghley Horse Trials in 1961 which combined his sporting interests and love of the estate and horses. Before the war he had been

[169] *above* The North Front of Burghley House in the Second World War. A German bomber, hastening home after a raid on Derby, jettisoned a 500-pound bomb which exploded in the park. The blast broke the glass of many windows and badly damaged the Tijou gates. The house had a lucky escape.

[170] *right* Shirley Slocombe, portraits of William, 5th Marquess of Exeter, and his wife Myra (Orde-Powlett), who kept Burghley, its estate and collections together during the difficult first half of the twentieth century. Lady Exeter compiled the first scholarly catalogue of the paintings in 1954.

[171] *below* William, 5th Marquess of Exeter, and Myra with (left to right) Romayne, Winifred, Martin and David, Lord Burghley, *c.* 1930.

Master of the Hounds in several countries. On returning to Burghley he restarted his own pack. He established the three-day event after he heard that the event at Harewood House in Yorkshire could no longer be held due to foot and mouth disease in the area. The course in Capability Brown's park was laid out by Bill Thompson who continued to supervise the course for over twenty years. The Horse Trials were an immediate success and have become the longest running international event, with many Championships including two World Championships in 1966 and 1974. The Horse Trials have been held every year since 1961, except during Covid in 2020 and 2021. Champion winners have included Princess Anne, Captain Mark Phillips, Lucinda Prior-Palmer and William Fox-Pitt. Phillips was the course designer from 1989 to 1996 and again in 1998. The Horse Trials have won many awards including the prestigious French L'Année Hippique on five occasions, a record. Burghley on the international sporting map added a new dimension to the estate, in tandem with the great Lord Burghley's architecture, the 5th Earl's collection of Italian paintings, the 9th Earl's landscaping by Capability Brown, and the 1st and 2nd Marquess's historical antiquarianism. It made the point that Burghley was still very much an active, living estate. The Trials attracted Royal visits, including Queen Elizabeth II and the Duke of Edinburgh in 1971. The three-day event has continued and grown into one of the most popular displays of horsemanship, attended by nearly two hundred thousand people annually. It has attracted successive sponsors, currently Land Rover.

Lord Exeter's principal tasks when he took over on his father's death in 1956 were tackling the run-down state of everything after two World Wars and a substantial bill for death duties, the first such tax demand since 1898 and assessed at 80 percent of the value of the estate, though there was reduced duty on agricultural land and the art collection was exempt as being of national artistic and historical interest. That, however, still left a substantial tax demand for all the other property. Outlying agricultural land had to be sold, as well as two major works of art: Poussin's *Assumption* via Wildenstein to the National Gallery of Art in Washington, D.C. and the late baroque sculpture of *Andromeda and the Sea Monster* by the Roman sculptor Domenico Guidi which had been bought by the 5th Earl and was for long the centrepiece of the Marble Hall. It is now in

[172] *opposite left* Oswald Birley, *David Cecil, 6th Marquess of Exeter*, in Cambridge blue athletes' blazer and shorts, painted in 1926.

[173] *opposite right* Lord Burghley, later 6th Marquess, as a champion Hurdler. He won the Gold Medal at the 1928 Olympics.

[174] *right* The Burghley Horse Trials were founded by the 6th Marquess in 1961 and have been an important part of the Burghley Year ever since.

[175] *below right* Queen Elizabeth II, Princess Margaret and Lord Exeter watching the Horse Trials from an improvised stand in the park.

[176] Nicolas Poussin, *The Assumption*. One of two major works of art from the Burghley collection sold by the 6th Marquess to pay death duties after the death of his father in 1956. As a result of these forced alienations, he set up policies to protect the house, collections and estate for the future. He set up a pioneering charitable preservation trust which assumed the management and preservation of Burghley after his death in 1981, carrying out an ambitious programme of restoration.

the Metropolitan Museum of Art in New York. Some china and silver were also sold including the Burghley Nef. To avoid such continuing attrition in the future, Lord Exeter set to thinking about transforming the collection to a trust to keep it all together regardless of family vicissitudes and political circumstances. In the 1960s he entered into negotiations with the National Trust, but these foundered over financial and management details, encouraging him to pursue the alternative option of an independent trust alongside continuing family occupation and management of the house, though at that stage only an educational trust seemed possible.

Death duties were only one of Lord Exeter's problems after inheriting the estate. There was also the worrying state of the house and its collections. The roof was leaking, the textiles falling to pieces, the paintings barely visible under dark varnish and the effluvia of a century's gas fumes. Burghley was probably the last major country house to install electric light. Cragside, Chatsworth, Hatfield and Arundel had all had electric light since the 1890s (as had the West End of London); most houses installed electric light just before or after the First World War, but in 1956 Burghley was still lit by gas and had no electricity. One of Lord Exeter's first tasks was to install mains electricity to the house. He also tackled some of the more pressing conservation problems, but like much 1960s restoration work there was an inclination towards using 'modern materials'. Thus, for instance, aluminium was used to replace some of the porous leadwork on the roof, cement rather than lime mortar, and 'rexine' rather than leather for re-upholstery. These contemporary 1960s 'solutions' soon created more problems than they solved and in due course all had to be replaced with traditional, organic materials, but at least efforts were made to revive the house. Lord Exeter's daughter Lady Victoria Leatham recalls her childhood, after they moved there in the 1950s, in her book *Burghley: The Life of a Great House* (1992). She describes her mother Diana's efforts to make it habitable and improve the showing to the public. 'Nobody had decorated much since World War I . . . Furniture was displayed in the most extraordinary way and everything needed repair. The many pictures that my grandfather had enthusiastically coated with . . . varnish were now black and shiny. There were tattered textiles and broken porcelain as far as the eye could see.' Money was short, however, and much of the presentation in the public rooms was stop gap. For instance, old guidebooks show cushions piled up against the foot of the state bed to disguise the decayed silk.

When Lord Exeter died in 1981 his plans for the Burghley House Preservation Trust came to fruition, and improved economic circumstances made possible more serious repairs. His brother Martin Cecil inherited the titles and became 7th Marquess of Exeter, but was long settled in Canada where the 5th Marquess had acquired land in British Columbia; his son Michael also lived in Canada. The new 7th Marquess ran an evangelical religious group there, the Emissaries of the Divine Light. So the trustees invited Lady Victoria Leatham, the 6th Marquess's daughter

[177] Raoul Martinez, *Michael, 8th Marquess of Exeter*. He succeeded his father in 1988. The present Marquess lives in Canada but visits Burghley regularly and takes an interest in its preservation.

by his second marriage, to become the 'house director', moving with her husband Simon and two children into the family apartments and running the place. It was always part of Lord Exeter's plan that the family presence should be maintained in the house. Lady Victoria was the obvious choice: She had grown up at Burghley, and then worked for Sotheby's for many years and had many connections among its experts as well as generally in the art world. She had both knowledge of the place and things, and useful contacts to tackle the conservation and display of the collections. There ensued what can only be described as a battle to save Burghley with a massive campaign to repair the structure, including renewal of all the roofs which involved one and a half acres of lead and Collyweston tiles, and conservation of the stone masonry of the walls, window mullions and the frilly roofscape, notably the seventy-six columnar chimneys which had been eroded by time and weather. Much of that structural work is not now noticeable because the repairs have been so well done and have now settled in so as to be hardly detectable.

The transformation of the interior was more immediately dramatic with the conservation and re-hang of the paintings, the repair and the gradual more authentic rearrangement of the furniture, and the conservation of seventeenth-century tapestries, bed hangings and other upholstery. The work inside the house was undertaken alongside a series of scholarly exhibitions of different facets of the collection, both at home and abroad, aimed at making it better-known and more available to a wider public. The conservation and exhibition programmes formed one holistic scholarly project based on detailed archival research. The exhibitions also made it possible to display the smaller, rarer objects, like the Japanese porcelain, Devonshire *Schatzkammer*, gold and silver plate, drawings, books and miniatures, which cannot all be permanently shown in the state rooms for conservation and security reasons. Behind-the-scenes specialist, secure storage was developed for much of this material after it was 'discovered', ranging from high-standard acid-free archive boxes for muniments, drawings and miniatures, to special store cupboards for the reserve porcelain collections. All this work was underpinned by wide historical research in the archives which produced fascinating information about the 5th Earl's and the 9th Earl's collections, travels, architectural alterations and improvements, ranging from inventories and original bills to correspondence with Italian dealers, and contemporary accounts of Grand Tours. Lady Victoria recognised the significance of the inventories and how the Japanese porcelain, for instance, could be identified in them, such as the 'China boys wrestling', adding enormously to its historic interest. Much of this detailed research was undertaken in-house by Dr. Eric Till of Stamford, who was honorary archivist at Burghley for many years until his death, and who trawled and published a mass of historical information making Burghley and its collections among the best understood in the country. His work has been continued, and digitized, by Jon Culverhouse who was appointed house-manager by Lady Victoria Leatham and has become the long-serving curator of the Burghley collections. This book is largely based on the discoveries and researches undertaken by Eric Till and Jon Culverhouse from the 1980s to the present day. The in-house expertise was complemented by continuous cooperation with various institutions, including the Ashmolean Museum at Oxford, and the art history departments at Warwick and Leicester universities, where a succession of research students have studied different aspects of the house and written detailed theses on subjects ranging from Lord Burghley's architecture to Stuart collecting, Verrio's painting and Georgian Grand Tours.

The immediate task in the 1980s was to tackle the structure, especially the roofs which were leaking in many places, and where Capability Brown's roof-fabric on the south front in particular gave alarming signs of imminent collapse with failing and rotten timbers. The 1950s electric wiring, much of it trailing along the surface, was also in need of complete renewal. A team was set up under the management of the then agent of the Burghley estate, Michael Scott. The architect chosen was Alan Wilson, in association with the structural engineer Alan Baxter, a leading specialist in historic buildings based in Clerkenwell, London, who was involved with a large range of important structures from Westminster Hall to Paddington Station. Wilson was the first of a series of consultant architects over the years who have prepared quinquennial structural reports and directed successive stages of repairs. The builders were Bowmans of Stamford, a family firm, originally of stone masons, established in the town for over a hundred years and specialists in conservation work until the company was dissolved in 2012; Bowmans were involved in many other important local projects including restoration at Lincoln Cathedral and Castle. Work on the renewal of the Burghley roofs began in 1983 and took fifteen years to complete. As well as renewing all the leadwork, melting down and reusing the old material on the main part of the house, the Collyweston roofs of the Great Hall, service court and stables were also redone, a mammoth task. The Collyweston quarry which has produced the eponymous stone tiles or slates since the Middle Ages is based on the estate, and part of the early workings are now a scheduled Ancient Monument and Site of Special Scientific Interest. In the 1990s and early 2000s the estate worked with English Heritage on new processes of maturing stone slates and reopening the quarry which had ceased working in the 1960s. This is one example of how the conservation programme at Burghley itself has had a wider impact on the preservation of historic buildings in England. Since then new-quarried Collyweston slates have been used not just at Burghley but at Apethorpe in Northamptonshire for English Heritage, Ufford church, and several Cambridge colleges. A complex moveable steel frame and corrugated iron cover, nicknamed the 'Burghley bird cage', was devised to protect the ceilings below while the lead was replaced. The structure of the Verrio ceilings was consolidated by stainless steel wires tied into a secondary layer of plaster applied above. The roof works at the house involved structural renewal as well as coverings. The re-roofing programme was part-funded with grants from English Heritage, making the house water-tight and protecting the rare baroque painted and stucco ceilings. Advantage was taken of modern technology such as installing electric wires in the gutters to thaw snow and ice and prevent blockages, and overflows of water.

The interior transformation was directed by Lady Victoria Leatham. She, with her husband Simon and two children, moved in to the family apartments, from their own home (forty miles away) at Alconbury in 1982 and systematically embarked on the conservation of the rooms and contents of Burghley. A priority was the picture collection where many of the paintings needed attention, and much of the hang was muddled, while wrong attributions abounded. The aim was to restore the spirit of the historic

[178] Simon and Lady Victoria Leatham in the Blue Drawing Room at Burghley, *c.* 1985.

hang as recorded in the 1688, 1738, '1763', and 1st Marquess's inventories, but respecting later adjustments of significance. A vast amount of conservation, cleaning and re-varnishing was required, and the distinctive Burghley House picture labels, a significant and personalised detail, were in need of re-gilding and re-numbering to take on board modern re-cataloguing of the collection which contains over seven hundred canvases, one of the largest accumulations in an English house, similar to Petworth, but double the size of the splendid historic collections at Wilton and Arundel.

John Somerville from the pictures department at Sotheby's was appointed honorary paintings curator to help sort things. He already knew the collection because when staying with the Leathams at Alconbury in 1979 he had been taken over to Burghley when Lord Exeter was still alive and had been shown round the paintings. From 1984 Lady Victoria and Somerville tackled the display, and he compiled his first hand-list of the collection as a visitors' guide in 1987 once the revised hang, with many new and corrected attributions, had reached a state where it was felt it could be described more definitively. In 1982 everything was muddled. Over the years pictures had been moved around and current favourites put in more prominent positions. Pairs and groups had been broken up and divided between the private apartments on the ground floor and the state apartments on the piano nobile. The task in hand did not involve just the moving of one or two canvases to better positions. The whole collection in every part of the house needed to be reconsidered, and pictures which were then on the ground floor had to be moved upstairs and vice versa. Together, Lady Victoria and Somerville sorted them all out and rearranged to produce a more historically authentic hang, inspired by old guidebooks and inventories. The aim was also to place the best pictures in prominent positions. This process could not be undertaken piecemeal because of the domino effect. The whole house had to be done in one campaign which encompassed the private as well as the public rooms; the works commissioned by the 9th Earl from Angelica Kauffman, for instance, were all assembled together in the Blue Drawing Room.

The pictures were not in physically bad condition, successive marquesses and their wives had looked after them, but nearly all were obscured by discoloured old varnish and a century of dirt and varnish. The 6th Marquess and his wife had employed Henry Happ, a German paintings restorer from Berlin who had come to England in 1933 and settled in Hampstead, following the rise of Hitler to power, but the varnish he used had discoloured over the intervening fifty years. Somerville recommended Alec Cobbe, who had recently trained as a picture restorer, to undertake the job, and a special on-site studio was installed in the east hall where Cobbe and his assistants could gently clean

[179] *right and far right* A Vanderbank tapestry in the Second George Room, commissioned by the 5th Earl and Countess. Washed and restored as part of the textile conservation programme overseen by the Landi Company established in the Stables.

and re-varnish the canvases, ready for re-hanging. Cobbe as well as conserving the paintings had a good eye and knowledge of art and historic collections, so he was also able to give advice, though Somerville master-minded the general disposition with an emphasis on the historic hang in the state rooms, making the more important items more visible to the public. Some re-framing and re-gilding was also undertaken and interesting old frames restored. As well as the work to the easel pictures in the 1980s, cleaning and conservation of the murals of Verrio and Laguerre was undertaken in the 1990s, with especially dramatic results, the original colours and quality of detail being revealed once more. This work was done by Michael Cowell and culminated in the ceiling of the Hell Staircase in 1993, following the Heaven Room. Laguerre's Bow Room was stabilised, cleaned and conserved in 1990, involving three thousand hours of craftsmen's time. This demonstrates the scale of the work involved.

The textiles, including tapestries and baroque bed hangings, were tackled in tandem with the art programme from 1982 onwards, starting with the sets of tapestry in the west wing ground and first floor rooms. The specialist Michael McGreal was in charge of this initially, and his workshop was established for the purpose on the estate. Sheila Landi from the Victoria and Albert Museum was the lead textiles consultant. The Mortlake *Bacchanals* in the Blue Silk Bedroom were the first to be cleaned and repaired and were followed by the Gobelins set by Jan Jans of the *Fables of La Fontaine*, and the Vanderbank *Elements*, and the Grotteschi set. In the early stages there was little funding for conservation of the things, though English Heritage grants were available towards the structural repairs of the roof and masonry. Lady Victoria and the trustees hit on the idea of outside sponsorship for specific restoration projects on the model of the Horse Trials. Thus Remy Martin who had sponsored the Horse Trials paid for the conservation of the seventeenth-century bed in the Queen Elizabeth Room in 1985, and the Cotton Trust paid towards renewing the silk of the state bed and window curtains of the Second George Room in 1988.

This sort of fundraising was tackled in the context of loan exhibitions abroad, in the United States and Japan. An exhibition of Burghley Japanese Kakiemon porcelain in association with Seibu Stores in Tokyo earned sponsorship for conservation of various items of furniture and paintings from that firm. Large and glamorous exhibitions in the United States raised awareness of the riches of the Burghley collection there and led to grants, for instance, to restore the Gole cabinet, prior to redisplay in the Blue Silk Bedroom after being rescued from a downstairs lobby. It had been badly damaged by woodworm. American Express contributed to book restoration, where over a thousand books were rebound. These loan exhibitions included the epochal *Treasure Houses of Britain* exhibition in 1985 at the National Gallery of Art in Washington, D.C., curated by Gervase Jackson-Stops who borrowed more from Burghley than from any other English country house. That was followed by *Italian Paintings from Burghley House*, an exhibition which toured the States in 1995 and 1996 and put the 5th Earl's collection in all its revived splendour back on the map. It was followed in 1999 by a large exhibition of treasures from across the full range of the collection, *The Cecil Family Collects*, with a scholarly catalogue by Oliver Impey, which is still the best introduction to the Burghley collection as a whole. These overseas loan exhibitions were held alongside smaller more focussed exhibitions at Burghley itself, drawing on current historical research and highlighting special aspects of the collection: Oriental ceramics, Chinese snuff bottles, portrait miniatures, metalwork and jewels from the Devonshire Bequest. These were at first held in the Goodie Rudkin Room in the courtyard near the kitchen entrance, but in 2006 it proved possible

to open a purpose-built visitor and education centre and treasury gallery in the Old Brew House which was restored and converted for the purpose as part of the general revival and re-use of subsidiary structures. This scheme was part funded by the Heritage Lottery, and designed by the architects Richard Griffiths and Partners. It won the Sandford Award, for education in country houses. The Oriental ceramics exhibitions drew on previous research by Gordon Lang which had established that the Burghley collection of the 5th Earl and his wife was the earliest, fully documented assemblage of imported Japanese and Chinese porcelain in Europe. Sheila Landi of the Victoria and Albert Museum became a key member of the Burghley conservation team over the decades, establishing a workshop in the stables in 1992 after she retired from the Museum, and her team has continued to look after the tapestries and beds down to the present. Richard Humphreys of Castle Hedingham has rewoven various silks to the original design and narrow loom patterns. Several specialist decorators as well as conservators have been involved. Their work includes the recreation of the painted marbled decoration in the first floor west rooms which was overseen by Lady Victoria Leatham. The Guild of Master Upholsterers, one of the City Livery Companies with a long association with the Exeter family, has restored over a dozen items of seat-furniture. Intricate marquetry, which was lifting badly on many pieces, has been restored by Paul Kelaart and Ian Palmer, and much general furniture restoration carried out by John Bly. Many of the conservators employed have been established in workshops on the estate over the years, where Capability Brown's stables, after many years of disuse, have been repaired, converted and let to craftsmen. This, as well as providing a pool of in situ expertise, is another example of the way in which the programme at Burghley has made a wider contribution to national and international conservation, for the craftsmen established there work elsewhere in the country, and take on and train new apprentices and specialists, keeping alive a range of valuable skills. Other craftsmen who have contributed included Toshi Iwata, a master carver; Alex Hammond, who refurbished the Devonshire *Kunstkammer*; Barry Witmond, who worked on the silver; and Michael Cowell, the resident paintings conservator. Another long-standing business is run by Anthony Beech, a craftsman, furniture conservator and restorer. His presence enables repairs to be carried out immediately before broken bits are lost. He has also been integral to many furniture discoveries that have been made.

Once the house and its contents were secure, the trustees and Lady Victoria were ready in the early 2000s to move on

to reviving the gardens, replanting the seventeenth-century avenues, and restoring the Capability Brown parkland. The north and south avenues have been replanted in sections, in order to maintain their form, using whips grown from the roots of the old lime trees in order to perpetuate the old species. The work started in 2003 and will be completed in 2025. The venerable trees in the park are of three main dates: sixteenth century, the George London Avenue trees, and Capability Brown's oaks, limes and sweet chestnuts. Few trees were planted in the park during the nineteenth and twentieth centuries, but a thousand have been planted in recent years, and one hundred thousand on the wider estate. The main modern introduction has been the creation of the Garden of Surprises, sited away from the Capability Brown landscape to the east of the stables. It was conceived by Lady Victoria Leatham as a twenty-first century contribution and opened in 2007. The garden was designed by George Carter and is a celebration of Elizabethan gardening and Lord Burghley's love of gardens as expressed in his works at Burghley and Theobalds. It was inspired by contemporary descriptions of the gardens at Theobalds which featured fountains and water features, a maze, grottoes, sundial, obelisks, trellis, statues and formal flower beds, symmetry and vistas. Elizabethan gardens were full of 'tricks and conceits' and expressed contemporary interests in astrology, mathematics, and astronomy as well as plants, horticulture, formal design, and renaissance classical civilisation. The Garden of Surprises comprises enclosed courts surrounded by hedges and trellis with vistas through and narrow canals and water features, an obelisk and sundial. It has become a popular additional feature for visitors to Burghley and is an example of how new work sympathetic to the spirit of the place can be introduced into the setting of historic buildings. The garden was in a way of being Lady Victoria Leatham's leaving present for Burghley, and in 2007 she retired as chatelaine of the house. The reins were taken up by her daughter Miranda who had studied art history at university and was married to Orlando Rock, Chairman of Christie's UK, and himself a great expert on historic art collections and English architecture. They moved into the house at the invitation of the trustees, with their young children, adapting the family rooms for contemporary life, creating a large family kitchen on the ground floor as the focus of daily living but respecting and enhancing the historic layouts. Whereas the previous generation of the family and trustees had concentrated on repairing the fabric of the house itself, and conserving the art collection and textiles, the programme now moved on to encompass the restoration of the Capability Brown park, and general landscape, and historic buildings on the estate. The redundant model dairy cottage in the park has been repaired with funding from the 6th Marquess of Exeter's Will Trust, and converted into holiday accommodation. The Bottle Lodges have also been restored, as has the Lion Bridge over the lake. The latter was an ambitious project in 2022. It is one of Burghley's biggest individual preservation projects in recent

[180] *opposite* The Treasury in the restored Brew House at Burghley, used for changing exhibitions of special treasures from the collection, with the Brew House as the educational centre.

[181] *below* Conservation underway in the workshops at Burghley. *Clockwise from top left*: Curator Jon Culverhouse re-gilding one of the flags that decorate the roofscape of the house; Mike Cowell, picture conservator; Barry Witmond, silversmith; Anthony Beech, furniture restorer.

[182] *above* Head Forester Peter Glassey, hedge-laying on the estate.

[183] *below* A visit from HM The Queen in 2012 to attend a Diamond Jubilee four-county picnic in the park.

years, and was partly made possible by the government's Culture Recovery Fund, set up to protect arts and heritage organisations in the aftermath of the Covid epidemic in 2020 and 2021. Across the country 142 heritage sites were selected for specific restoration work. Capability Brown's bridge at Burghley received a grant of £400,000, and the trustees put in £110,000 from estate reserves. The work was directed by the estate's own team and local contractors under David Pennell who came in to run the Burghley estate from Arundel. The bridge structure was being damaged by water percolating down from the parapets and road surface into the lower structure threatening its stability. As well as masonry repairs and repointing, a modern tarmac road surface was removed and replaced with stone sets on a waterproof base, which improves the appearance of the bridge by giving a more traditional finish.

Extensive landscape restoration has also been undertaken in the park, to open up and enhance Capability Brown's landscape under the direction of the Burghley Head Forester Peter Glassey who is a leading expert on trees and has worked at Burghley since 1992. Modern plantations that blocked vistas have been removed, historic trees and Brown's plantings protected and reinstated where possible, and structural repairs have been made to buildings like the massive brick walls of the kitchen garden which had fallen into disrepair. Arable land formerly within the Capability Brown layout has been returned to parkland and the historic park curtilage of thirteen hundred acres reinstated with sheep reintroduced in 2018. Similar landscape restoration has also been undertaken on the wider estate, notably the renewal of traditional hedges, laying them in the Midland style using hazel sticks and binders, perpetuating a local craft. (Different parts of England have their own styles of hedge-laying; the Cotswolds for instance being different from the Lake District.) The park landscape restoration has also involved the moving of the visitors' car park to a

[184] *above* A Roman marble bust of a lady, Second Century CE, mounted on a seventeenth-century socle, which was unearthed in the park in 2023.

site further east of the house where it sits more comfortably in the layout. The former car park was obtrusive in first views from the approach and was also damaging the roots of historic trees, so its removal is an improvement both in visual and arboricultural terms.

In addition, the gardens and pleasure grounds have been greatly enhanced under Miranda Rock's direction, with judicious new planting and improvement, and removal of overgrowth, by Head Gardener Joe Whitehead and his team. More exotic trees have been planted there including cedars, deodars, pines and cork oaks. Significant rearrangements of the furniture within the house have been undertaken and now complement the 1980s and 1990s revival of the traditional picture hang. Sets of furniture have been put together again; and more balanced and symmetrical groupings achieved. Damaged pieces from store have continued to be conserved and reinstated in their historic locations. Many of these more recent adjustments, which have been undertaken with the advice of Orlando Rock, are subtle and are not immediately apparent, but are nevertheless significant. The sculpture, for instance, has been concentrated in the Hell Stairs, including the Monnot busts of the 5th Earl and Countess, and the 9th Earl's commissions from Nollekens, but also a number of Roman antiquities including funerary urns and portrait busts which had been acquired by the 9th Earl. A significant addition to the latter is a classical bust of a Roman woman discovered in the ground when excavating the new car park in 2023 where it had been buried for hundreds of years. This is the most dramatic of the discoveries that have continued to be made. Others include a fine eighteenth-century desk, obviously one of the 9th Earl's furniture commissions, which was noticed in the estate office and retrieved to become the centrepiece of the Pagoda Room, where it keeps company with the Angelica Kauffman portrait of the 9th Earl commissioned by him in Naples when on the Grand Tour, which he bequeathed to his sister Lady Betty at Snape Castle in Yorkshire and which had come onto the market and was bought for the Burghley collection. Another recent addition is a pastel portrait by John Russell of Lady Betty herself, which was recognised in a local saleroom by Orlando Rock and bought for Burghley. Floorboards have been revealed and polished and new LED picture lighting installed, and the research programme continued. John Somerville published an updated catalogue of the paintings in 2007.

Increasing emphasis is being placed on education and attracting new audiences, and explaining the architecture and art collections to young children. Management of the surrounding estate prioritises restoration of the historic landscape and wild life, recognising the importance of the Sites of Special Scientific Interest like the quarry workings at Collyweston, some managed in-house, and some by English Nature. The Trust is also keen to ensure that new building developments on estate land in and around Stamford enhance the town's fine architectural heritage. This is demonstrated by the redevelopment of the old football ground near the railway station, recently completed, where stone-built townhouses have been planned by Hugh Petter of Adam Architecture. A similar but larger scheme for Stamford North (adjoining the new sports grounds

[185] *below* A sketch of the Stamford North development by the master-planner Hugh Petter of Adam Architecture.

[186] *opposite* Burghley continues as a family home being lived in by the family of Lord Exeter's daughter Lady Victoria Leatham, and now his grand-daughter, Miranda Rock. They are the resident curators of Burghley House. As well as continuing its conservation, they add to the collections, redisplay objects to advantage, and organise special exhibitions.

developed there by the Trust with the Sports Lottery) is planned in the same way and will provide a future endowment for Burghley enabling it to be maintained to the highest standards for many years to come.

A major direction for the future is the management of the natural environment of the whole estate which comprises around twelve thousand acres, with a home farm of eighteen hundred acres. When the 6th Marquess set up the charitable trust one of the aims was to conserve, and restore for the benefit of the nation, the natural environment of the property held by the Trust and to promote ecologically sustainable practises in estate management thereon. In this, as in so much else, Lord Exeter was a pioneer. In 2010 Professor Sir John Lawton published a government review into the management of ancient woodland, wildlife and farming in England, which revealed the fragmentation of ecological networks within the English landscape. Isolated nature reserves provided islands in a sea of intensive farming and building development. There was a need for a larger-scale more sustainable, holistic approach which old landed estates like Burghley are able to provide and develop. To this end James Tusting has been taken on to plan new proposals for nature protection and sustainable farming. The aim is to protect the health of the soil and make space for nature while continuing food production and maintaining farm profitability. As well as more conservation-orientated management of Burghley's own farms, the Charitable Trust is cooperating with neighbouring land owners on larger-scale landscape recovery, notably the John Clare Countryside Project which it is hoped will provide a substantial restoration of the wider Middle England landscape outside the park, retaining historic features and protecting and enhancing wild life.

The house and park and wider estate now show the benefits of forty years of careful management and conservation by the family and trustees. Burghley is today not just a marvellous survival of English Elizabethan architecture with a magnificent baroque interior and art collection, but also a model of how historic houses, landscapes and collections should be looked after and displayed, and it remains a happy family home, as well as one of the great historic show places of Europe.

[188] Table-scape in the Red Drawing Room with Bassano's *Adoration of the Magi* above Bouke de Vries' contemporary Guanyin sculpture.

[189] Re-created historic display of Chinese and Japanese porcelain on the tiered chimneypiece in the Blue Silk Dressing Room.

[190] Objects collected by Miranda and Orlando Rock in the Marble Hall, alongside conjoined twin lambs, born in Burghley Park in the late nineteenth century and re-fleeced in the Army and Navy Stores in London in 1959.

[191] Shells and coral arranged on the small Florentine cabinet in a corridor on the ground floor.

[192] The Pagoda Room. The handsome mahogany desk attributed to Mayhew and Ince was rescued from the Estate Office, and recently placed here as the centrepiece of the furnishings.

[193] The Red Drawing Room—*Venus and Adonis* by Giovanni Battista Gaulli, Il Baciccio (1639–1709), first mentioned in the 1738 Inventory and probably bought by the 5th Earl of Exeter on the Grand Tour in 1699, hanging above a late-seventeenth-century Antwerp Cabinet with Flemish painted scenes and an Andrew Wickes ceramic garniture.

[194] A Closet off the Pagoda Room. These closets were converted into a bathroom and dressing room in the late-nineteenth century.

[195] The Ante Library, with a display of the younger generation's artistic endeavours.

[196] A family bedroom.

[197] The library on the ground floor, with the portrait by Sir Thomas Lawrence of the third wife of the 1st Marquess. It is now also used as the formal dining room.

[198] The South Bedroom and bathroom—part of the suite of rooms occupied by Anne, wife of the 5th Earl.

[199] *previous pages* The North Front of Burghley House.

[200] *left* The South Gardens with restored fountains and new water jet introduced into the lake in 2015.

[201] *previous pages* Lone fallow buck under Capability Brown's oak trees, with glimpses of the west front. The herd of deer is a historic feature of the park, having been introduced by Lord Burghley in 1562.

[202] Astrological feature in the Garden of Surprises, designed by George Carter for Lady Victoria Leatham.

[203] Water channel in the Garden of Surprises developed by Lady Victoria Leatham, inspired by descriptions of Lord Burghley's famous lost gardens at his other house Theobalds, in Hertfordshire, which was destroyed during the English Civil War in the seventeenth century.

[204] The Hidden Towers of the 'Hide and Secrets' adventure playground, designed by CapCo, which opened in 2023.

[205] The Sculpture Garden with *From Far Away Great Changes Come As Forms You Thought You Knew* by Robert Fung.

[206] *following pages* Rick Kirby's *Vertical Face II* amidst wild flowers in the Sculpture Garden, a visitor attraction which covers twelve acres in the pleasure grounds.

[207] A view across the lake toward the West Front at Burghley in the afternoon sun.

[208] The north forecourt, with a statue of the Young Bacchus purchased by the 9th Earl in Italy.

[209] *left* Aerial view showing the restored Queen Anne's avenue in the High Park as part of the evolving parkland management plan. The lake, Capability Brown's 'new river', can be seen winding through the garden.

[210] *following pages* Winter morning across the lake with a view to *Stag* by Sally Matthews.

—Appendices—

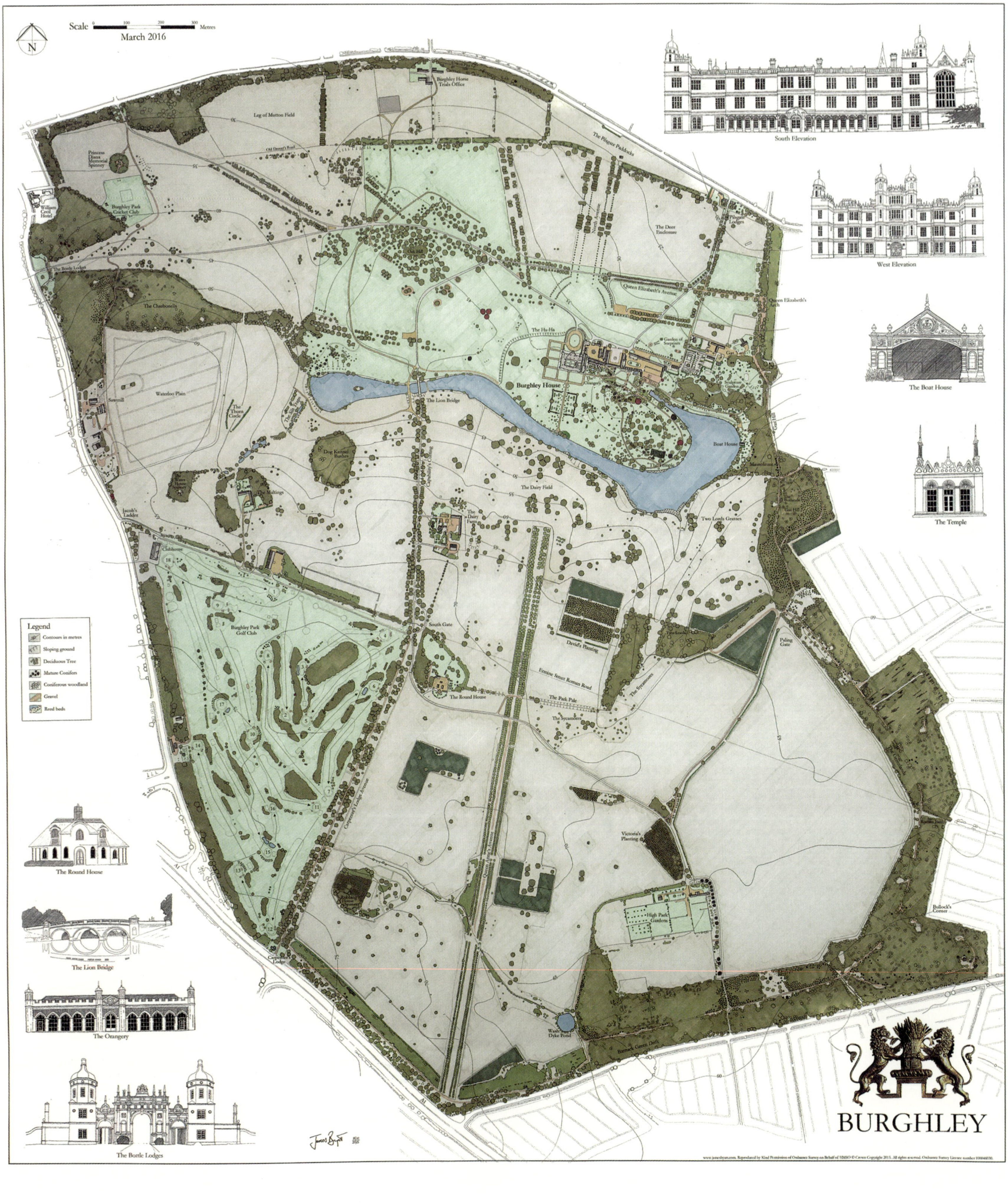

N
Scale
Metres
March 2016
Burghley House Trials Office
Leg of Mutton Field
The Pilsgate Paddocks
Princess Diana Memorial Spinney
Burghley Park Cricket Club
William Cecil Hotel
The Bottle Lodges
The Deer Enclosure
Queen Elizabeth's Avenue
The Charbonells
The Ha-Ha
Burghley House
Waterloo Plain
Sawmill
The Thorn Circle
The Lion Bridge
Dog Kennel Bushes
The Maltings
The Dairy Field
The Dairy Farm
Boat House
Two Lords Grasses
Jacob's Ladder
Clubhouse
Burghley Park Golf Club
South Gate
David's Planting
Ermine Street Roman Road
The Round House
The Park Pale
The Sycamores
Paling Gate
Victoria's Planting
High Park Gardens
Bullock's Corner
Carpenter's Lodge
Dyke Pond
A1
Legend
Contours in metres
Sloping ground
Deciduous Tree
Mature Conifers
Coniferous woodland
Gravel
Reed beds
South Elevation
West Elevation
The Boat House
The Temple
The Round House
The Lion Bridge
The Orangery
The Bottle Lodges
BURGHLEY

The Cecils of Burghley

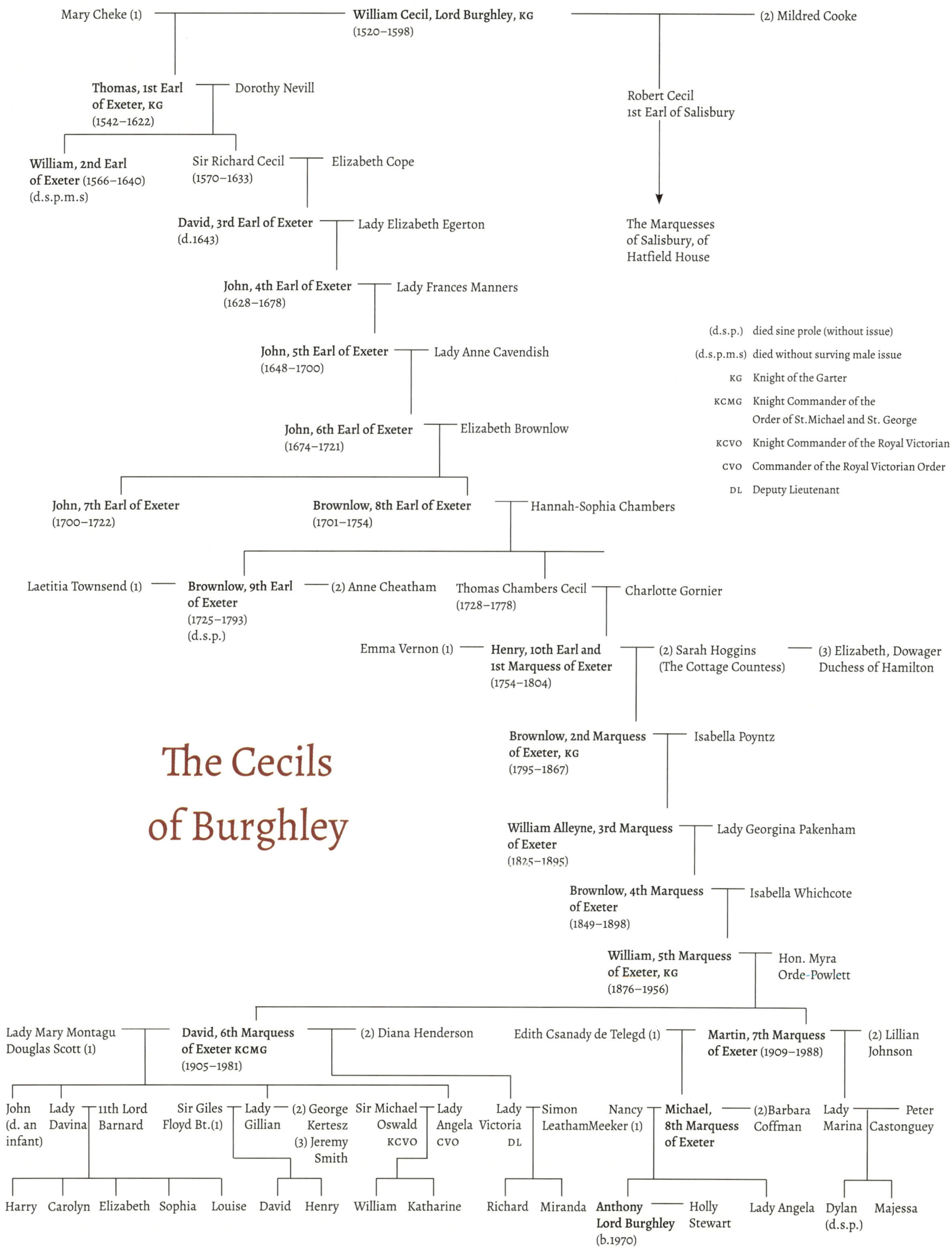

(d.s.p.)	died sine prole (without issue)
(d.s.p.m.s)	died without surving male issue
KG	Knight of the Garter
KCMG	Knight Commander of the Order of St.Michael and St. George
KCVO	Knight Commander of the Royal Victorian Order
CVO	Commander of the Royal Victorian Order
DL	Deputy Lieutenant

Selected Bibliography: Burghley House

A Guide to Burghley House (London: English Life/Heritage House Publications, 2009).

Abel & Sons, *The Progress and Visit... of Queen Victoria... to Burghley* (1844).

Stephen Alford, *Burghley: William Cecil at the Court of Elizabeth I* (New Haven: Yale University Press, 2008).

John Blore, *A Guide to Burghley House, Northamptonshire, the Seat of the Marquis of Exeter* (London: John Drakard, 1815).

Edward Chaney ed., *The Evolution of English Collecting* (London: Yale University Press, 2004).

Rev. W. Charlton, *The Life of William Cecil, Lord Burghley... A Description of Burghley House, Stamford* (Stamford: W. Langley, 1847).

Pauline Croft (ed.), *Patronage, Culture and Power—The Early Cecils, 1558–1612* (New Haven: Yale University Press, 2002).

David Esterley, *Grinling Gibbons and the Art of Carving* (London: V & A Publishing, 1998).

W. Harrod, *The Antiquities of Stamford and St Martin's* (Stamford: Harrod, 1785).

J. Horn, A *History or Description of Burghley House* (London: J. & W. Eddowes, 1797).

Celia Fiennes, *The Illustrated Journeys* (ed. Christopher Morris (London: MacDonald & Co., 1982).

Gerald Gifford, *A Descriptive Catalogue of the Music Collection at Burghley House* (Aldershot: Ashgate Publishing, 2002).

Mark Girouard, *Elizabethan Architecture* (London: Yale University Press, 2009).

Jillian Husselby, *The Architecture of Burghley House: the patronage of William Cecil, 1553–1598* (PhD thesis University of Warwick, 1996).

John Ingamells, *Dictionary of British & Irish Travellers in Italy 1701–1800* (London: Yale University Press, 1997).

Victoria Leatham, *Burghley, The Life of a Great House* (London: The Herbert Press, 1992).

Amy Lim, *Art & Aristocracy in late Stuart England* (D.Phil thesis of Oxford University, 2021).

David Loades, *The Cecils: Privilege and Power behind the Throne* (Kew: The National Archives, 2006).

John Fitzhugh Millar, *Hendrik van Paesschen, Architect of the Northern European Renaissance* (MA thesis William and Mary College, VA, 1981).

Hugh Roberts and Charles Cator, *Industry and Ingenuity: the Partnership of William Ince and John Mayhew* (London: Philip Wilson Publishers, 2022).

John Somerville and Jon Culverhouse, *Burghley: A Guide to the Paintings* (Peterborough: Jarrold Publications, 2019).

C. Stead, *Investigation into the Patronage and Collection of Italian Art in 17th Century England with Particular Reference to the Life and Collection of John Cecil, the 5th Earl of Exeter at Burghley* House (MA thesis Birkbeck College).

A Thomas, *Richard Creed's Journal of the Grand Tour 1699–1700* (Peterborough: Oundle Museum Trust, 2002).

Eric Till, *A Family Affair, Stamford and the Cecils, 1650–1900*. (A.H. Jolly (Editorial), 1990).

Selected Bibliography: The Burghley House Collection

CATALOGUES OF EXHIBITIONS HELD AT BURGHLEY HOUSE:

'The Wrestling Boys,' Chinese and Japanese Export Porcelain, 1983, curated by Gordon Lang.

'The Burghley Silver,' 1984, curated by John Webster.

'The Countess's Gems,' 16th & 17th Century Jewels, Gems and Objects of Vertu, 1985, curated by Anna Somers Cocks.

'European Ceramics at Burghley House,' 1991, curated by Gordon Lang.

LOAN EXHIBITION CATALOGUES

'*Chinese Snuff Bottles from the Burghley House Collection, Stamford, England*,' 1989, curated by Robert Kleiner.

'*The Burghley Porcelains*,' catalogue by Hiroko Nishida and others (New York: Japan House Gallery, 1986.)

'*Da un antico castello Inglese*,' catalogue by Roberto Valeriani (Milan: La Rinascente, 1994).

'*Italian Paintings from Burghley House*,' catalogue by Hugh Brigstocke and John Somerville (Alexandra, VA: Art Services International, 1995).

'*The Cecil Family Collects—Four centuries of Decorative Arts from Burghley* House,' catalogue by Oliver Impey (Alexandra, VA: Art Services International, 1998).

'*Export Lacquer: Reflection of the West in Black & Gold Makie*,' (Osaka: The Yomiuri Shimbun). Exhibitions at the Kyoto National Museum and the Suntory Museum, Tokyo, Oct 2008—Jan 2009.

SELECTED ARTICLES

Reinier Baarsen,'Mix and Match Marquetry,' *Country Life*, 13 October 1988.

Adam Bowett, 'The Floral Marquetry Floor at Burghley House,' *Burlington Magazine*, August 2022.

John Cornforth,'An Eye for Extravagance,' *Country Life*, 7 April 1988.

Giles Ellwood,'Burghley House, Lincolnshire,' *Country Life*, 28 September 1995.

Mark Girouard 'Elizabethan architecture and the Gothic tradition,' *Architectural History*, Volume 6, 1963.

Mark Girouard,'Burghley House, Lincolnshire—I, II,' *Country Life*, 30 April 1992.

Mark Girouard,'The Baiting of Burghley,' *Country Life*, 31 May 1990.

Christopher Hussey,'Burghley House, Northamptonshire—I, II, III, IV, V,' *Country Life*, 31 December 1953.

Gervase Jackson-Stops,'Battling for Burghley,' *Country Life*, 12 May 1988.

Eric Till,'A Furniture Discovery at Burghley,' *Country Life*, 7 June 1973.

Eric Till,'Decked in Splendour,' *Country Life*, 13 June 1991.

Eric Till, 'Capability Brown at Burghley', *Country Life*, 16 October 1975.

Eric Till,'The Development of the Park and Gardens at Burghley,' *Garden History Society*, Autumn 1991.

Endnotes

1 Is it fanciful to think Hawksmoor would have seen Burghley when travelling up the Great North Road to Castle Howard?

2 Jennifer Alexander, *Burghley House. The Roman Stair*. Report 2015

3 John Fitzhugh Millar, *Hendrik van Paesschen, Architect of the Northern European Renaissance*'. MA Thesis, William and Mary College, Virginia (1981)

4 'An Inventory of the Goods in Burghley House belonging to the Rt. Honble John Earl of Exeter and Ann Countess of Exeter, Taken August 28th 1688'.

5 'Conveyance and Schedule of Gift', 18 April 1690.

6 David Esterley *Grinling Gibbons and the Art of Carving* (1998) pp.93–5

7 William Harrod *Antiquities of Stamford* (1785)

8 Joan D'Arcy, 'Exeter House, Derby', *Derbyshire Miscellany*', vol.21 (2016) pp.2, 13

9 Hugh Roberts and Charles Cator, *Industry and Ingenuity* (2002) p.89

10 He did, however, buy the remarkable bronze head 'The Arundel Homer' from Dr. Meade's sale in London and gave it to the British Museum in 1760.

11 *The Progress and Visit of Her Most Gracious Majesty Queen Victoria and Her Royal Consort to the Princely Hospitality of Burghley* (Abel & Sons, 1844)

Index

[211] *following pages* Burghley staff in the North Court, February 2025.

First published in the United States of America in 2025 by
Rizzoli International Publications, Inc.
49 West 27th Street
New York, NY 10001

www.rizzoliusa.com

Archival imagery courtesy of the Burghley House Preservation Trust Ltd.
Drawings p. 32 © Sir John Soane's Museum, London
Map p. 258 by James Byatt, 2015

Designed by Robert Dalrymple
Set in Juan Pablo del Peral's Alegreya typeface

Publisher: Charles Miers
Editor: Jacob Lehman
Copy Editor: Sarah Stump
Proofreaders: Andrea Danese, Tricia Levi
Production Manager: Gloria Arminio
Managing Editor: Lynn Scrabis

Printed in China

MIX
Paper | Supporting responsible forestry
FSC™ C005748

2025 2026 2027 2028 / 10 9 8 7 6 5 4 3 2 1
ISBN: 978-0-8478-7554-2
Library of Congress Control Number: 2025934667

The authorized representative in the EU for product safety and compliance is Mondadori Libri S.p.A., via Gian Battista Vico 42, Milan, Italy, 20123, www.mondadori.it